Courage To Be An Entrepreneur

Courage To Be An Entrepreneur

◆

When You Are Flat Broke

Claiming territory for the kingdom of God through business ownership

Freda Wallace

iUniverse, Inc.
New York Lincoln Shanghai

Courage To Be An Entrepreneur
When You Are Flat Broke

iUniverse books may be ordered through booksellers or by contacting:

iUniverse
2021 Pine Lake Road, Suite 100
Lincoln, NE 68512
www.iuniverse.com
1-800-Authors (1-800-288-4677)

ISBN: 978-0-595-44452-6 (pbk)
ISBN: 978-0-595-88779-8 (ebk)

Printed in the United States of America

This book is dedicated to my father, the late Rev. Fred T Rooters. Ordained as a minister at the age of sixteen, he had the courage to leave the cotton fields of Pine Bluff, Arkansas in the 1950s. He went on to become a successful entrepreneur and a mighty man of God. He transferred from labor to reward in 2001. He left behind a rich legacy for his children, grandchildren, and the countless other lives he touched.

Contents

Acknowledgement

First, I thank God for his love manifested to us through His son and my redeemer Jesus Christ. I thank my family whom I love dearly. I thank my pastor Bishop TD Jakes and First Lady Serita Jakes for all that they do. I thank my friends on the evangelism team at the Potter's House for allowing me to co-labor with them, and carry the gospel to our inner city. I thank my many customers for your love and financial support.

Preface

Have you ever heard a really good sermon or song that challenged you to change something about your life, but later realized it was harder than you thought? Most of us have good intentions, but change is challenging. However if you are ever going to start, you just have to start. If you start with small baby steps, get up every time you fall down, you will learn to walk. This book is about encouraging you to try.

Change does not come without education. Your education must be aimed at where you are going. Education starts in the spirit, and then flows forth into the earth to rise up as an agent of change to achieve its intended purpose. Jesus said the Holy Spirit will teach us all things. In Matthew 6:33 He said it this way, *But seek ye first the kingdom of God, and his righteousness; and all these things shall be added unto you.*

Economists tell us that 70% of the wealth in this country is controlled by 9% of the population. The bottom 25% of the population has become poorer and poorer over the last twenty-five years. Many people in the middle face mounting debt and an uncertain future. Entrepreneurship is about leveling the playing field. It does not matter where you start. It matters where you finish.

This book is for people who want to aim at a better life for themselves through entrepreneurship. It is about the beginning phase of creating a business and answers the question how do I start when I am broke. The goal is to help you understand that before you can build a skyscraper you have to dig down deep and lay a solid foundation. When you operate effectively in the kingdom of God, you build on a strong foundation that enables you to withstand the storms of life.

God bless you on your venture

1

The Foundation

But seek ye first the kingdom of God,
and his righteousness;

and all these things shall be added unto you.

Matthew 6:33

In The Beginning

When I was four years old, my mother died. My father was left alone with four little children to raise. He made a decision to start his own business. That was in the 1960s during the height of the civil rights movement. There was a riot in our city. Most of the businesses in our area were burned down or severely vandalized. My father owned the only African American business in the area. Our business was left completely untouched.

I grew up as an entrepreneur in a family of entrepreneurs. **One question I heard my whole life was, "How do I start my own business?"** After a while, I realized that most people do not really want to know the answer to that question. What they really want to know is how to skip all the grunge work, the days of being broke, the long hours, the painful learning process and simply reap the harvest. My answer to that is, owning a business is not a get rich quick scheme. You will reap what you sow. That usually gets a less than enthusiastic response. The planting season is hard because there is so much to learn, but overtime the process does get easier and the money does come. You will have the autonomy to build according to your values, goals, and dreams. Owning a business is not like a job. It is a valuable equity building investment, which can pass from generation to generation. If built on a solid foundation, it will stand the storms of life.

In Matthew 7:24-29, Jesus said it this way:

Therefore whosoever heareth these sayings of mine, and doeth them, I will liken him unto a <u>wise</u> man, which built his house upon a rock:

And the rain descended, and the floods came, and the winds blew, and beat upon that house; and it fell not: for it was founded upon a rock.

And every one that heareth these sayings of mine, and doeth them not, shall be likened unto a <u>foolish</u> man, which built his house upon the sand:

And the rain descended, and the floods came, and the winds blew, and beat upon that house; and it fell: and great was the fall of it.

And it came to pass, when Jesus had ended these sayings, the people were astonished at his doctrine:

For he taught them as one having authority, and not as the scribes.

The only difference Jesus described between the two houses was the foundation. Both men were builders. He called the man who built on sand foolish. Why would anyone build a house on sand? Is it cheaper than rock? Is it easier to build on sand than rock? What is sand? Sand is not liquid. You can stand on sand. It appears solid. It apparently was solid enough to build a house on. Both houses may have even lasted for quite some time.

Jesus said that it was not until the rains descended, and the floods came, and the winds blew, that the problem with the foundation was revealed. The house built on the rock did not fall. The house built on the sand fell *and great was the fall.* He said whosoever heareth these sayings of mine, and doeth them, I will liken him unto a wise man, and whosoever heareth these sayings of mine, and doeth them *not,* shall be liken unto a foolish man. **Both men heard what Jesus was saying. The wise man *did* what Jesus said. The foolish man *did not.***

I have observed many would be entrepreneurs get a few dollars together, rent a retail space, buy some inventory, hang out an open sign and hope to get rich. Most simply went broke. Others cashed out their 401k plans and the equity in their homes to buy franchises, and still went broke. These are tragic situations. Most have felt so humiliated they never tried again.

The scripture above says *the people were astonished at his doctrine: For he taught them as one having authority, and not as the scribes.* Jesus talked and walked among the people. He looked like one of them, but they were astonished by what He said and how He said it. He is still speaking and teaching with authority today, and often through ordinary looking people. If you allow Him to be your foundation, you will be astonished at what He will speak into your life.

This book is about the beginning phase of how to start a business when you are broke. Long before you rent a retail space, qualify for a bank loan, or even have the support of the people around you, there are critical lessons that you need to learn. We will lay a solid foundation to enable your business to withstand the rains, the floods, and the winds of life. **Think of it this way, you have to learn the alphabet before you can learn to read.** This is an alphabet class for entrepreneurs.

THE POWER OF GOD

This book was originally developed as part of an evangelism/discipleship course. **We will talk a lot about God, because ultimately it is the power of God that causes us to prosper**. He is our foundation. The remainder of this chapter is devoted to understanding how God is our foundation. If we build our lives according to God's plan, we will achieve and sustain success. Christian entrepreneurs are successful, because we are kingdom builders. Your business will succeed when you understand that you are a builder in the kingdom of God. Daniel 11:32 says, *but the people that do <u>know</u> their God shall be strong and do exploits.*

God is not a fool. He does not tell us that we can do great things, just so He can watch us fail. He does not want us to fail. He wants us to succeed, but He knows that we will fail depending on ourselves. The systems of this world operate out of scarcity rather than abundance.

People are in competition with each other instead of cooperation. The message is that resources are limited and you better go out and get yours before there is nothing left. Whoever gets there first gets the best. The amount of money you have determines your position in line. People are encouraged to watch the ones ahead of them fall, and are rewarded by how quickly they can step over them and take their position. We are born into this negative system, and taught the rules from an early age. The older we get, the more the pressure mounts.

Then we, as a society, engage in all sorts of dysfunctional behaviors to try to cope. Mostly, we are simply confused, hurt, and angry. We tried our best to play by the rules but still could not win. The rules kept changing.

The more we struggled to get ahead the further behind we got. Even if you appear to be doing all right today, there is always the threat that some catastrophe can happen, and you can lose it all. An undertone of anxiety, fear, and insecurity is prevalent throughout our world. We fight against each other for a worthless prize. The problem is that no one wins. The systems of this world were designed only to kill, steal, and destroy. It kills our spirit, steals our joy, and destroys our hope.

Jesus came to tell us that the only way to win is to flip the script. Instead of mindlessly following the system that is working against you, you have to wake up. You do not need to buy another house, or car, or more clothes, or go back to school, or even start a business before you understand that there are two systems operating at the same time. The first one we are born into *without* a choice. The second one we are born into *with* a choice. If we make no choice, or do not understand that there is even a choice to make, then we live out our entire lives in the first system.

There is better system, however, and many people have already found it. It is the kingdom of God. The good news that Jesus brought to us is that the kingdom of God is here. He restored it to us as it was originally intended it to be, before the fall of man. It now is in all born again believers. However, people are still sleep walking, not truly living, but merely existing in that fallen, fallible system. Unfortunately, they are working harder and harder at it, hoping against hope that things will get better.

There is abundance not lack in the kingdom of God. We have what we need. There is no reason to lie, cheat, or steal to get ahead of anyone. We do the opposite. We welcome anyone who will hear and receive the call to wake up. There is plenty for all. God wants us to learn from Him and operate in faith and love. We walk and talk with a living God just as He walked and talked with Adam and Eve in the Garden of Eden. **We are not passive and weak. We are bold and decisive. We possess real power.** We know that our kingdom makes perfect sense. We are the children of God and we are learning and growing in the image of our Father every day.

The Gospel of St. John 1:1-14 says:

In the beginning was the Word, and the Word was with God, and the Word was God.

The same was in the beginning with God.

All things were made by Him; and without him was not any thing made that was made.

In Him was life; and the life was the light of men.

And the light shineth in the darkness; and the darkness comprehended it not.

There was a man sent from God, whose name John.

The same came for a witness, to bear witness of the Light, that all men through him might believe.

He was not that Light, but was sent to bear witness of that light

That was the true light, which lighteth every man that cometh into the world.

He was in the world, and the world was made by Him, and the world Knew Him not.

He came unto His own, and His own received him not.

But as many as received Him, to them gave He <u>power to become</u> the sons of God, even to them that believed on his name:

Which were born, not of blood, nor of the will of the flesh, nor the will of man, but of God.

And the Word was made flesh, and dwelt among us, (and we beheld his glory, the glory as of the only begotten of the Father,) full of grace and truth.

We have a clear and divine purpose. We are points of light scattered throughout a dark and sleeping world. **The kingdom of God is on the**

move. We are growing every day. We are touching lives and people are waking up. We are a powerful kingdom lead by a powerful king.

Entry into this kingdom is heavily guarded and protected. Jesus said no one could come in except through Him. He is the gatekeeper, and He judges the intent of the heart. Anyone who wants to come in must believe in Him and ask Him. No one else can let anyone in or out. I will say that again. No one else can let anyone in or out. No one gets in by going to church, reading the bible, or being a good person. Those things are good and needed but the only way to enter His kingdom is to receive Him as the Son of God. There is no form or fashion to follow.
Simply,

- Believe that He is who He said He is
- Believe that He can do what He said He could do
- Receive Him into your heart.

Then,

- He will allow you into His kingdom
- You will no longer be at the mercy of this world's system
- You will be a child of God.
- You will wake up a little more and more each day
- You will grow into your new life in the kingdom of God.

LIVING IN THE KINGDOM OF GOD

Let us look at the analogy of moving from one city to another, such as from Milwaukee to Dallas. Let us say that you lived in Milwaukee your whole life. Then, one day you decide to move to Dallas. Dallas is unfamiliar at first. The streets are different. The neighborhoods are different and even the food and speech is different. Dallas is a much bigger city in land area and population. You discover that Dallas is already up and running. It did not just start when you got there. Many people live there and have for quite some time. Nor did Milwaukee cease to exist because you moved. The two cities exist at the same time and will continue to do so.

There are some familiar things about Dallas. It has a central downtown district like Milwaukee. It has suburbs and malls. There are parks and schools. There are people. People have jobs and businesses. People drive cars and live in houses. There is a system of government, and there is an economic system.

Moving to Dallas, does not mean you are no longer you. You still wear clothes although they are different. You need more warm weather than cold weather clothes. You still need sleep, food, and money. If you were a doctor in Milwaukee, Dallas needs doctors. You learn the rules for Dallas and transfer your license from Wisconsin to Texas. If you were an entrepreneur in Milwaukee, your skills and talents are still valid and useful in Dallas. You find an opportunity and build a business. If you were a bus driver in Milwaukee, and you want to continue to drive buses, Dallas has a flourishing market for bus drivers. You study the map of Dallas, learn the new streets and laws, and get a Texas license.

If your map still has Lake Michigan on it, you are using the wrong map. That is OK. Sometimes it takes a while to remember that you are in a new city. At first, you measure all of your new experiences against the old. You say things like, "in Milwaukee we did it this way or that way," or "Milwaukee has a better this or that," or "I sure miss this or that about Milwaukee." Dallas is still unfamiliar and strange. We have a way of romanticizing our memories. Remembering only the good times and not the bad, but the longer you stay in Dallas the more distant Milwaukee becomes. It will never go completely away, because there are good things about Milwaukee. Your life experiences that you brought with you to Dallas are important and useful.

Of course, I am not really talking about Dallas or Milwaukee. Neither Dallas nor Milwaukee is better or worse than the other is. **I am talking about transitioning from the systems of this world into the kingdom of God.** Here, there is a profound difference. You cannot get in your car and drive there. It comes on the inside of you when you are born again. It enters us, and we enter it.

The kingdom of God is alive and flourishing. It permeates throughout the whole world through the children of God. We do not enter into the kingdom and leave behind everything about our lives. We are a spirit, still living in a body and we have a soul. The bible says we are in the world but not of the world. It is important to remember that we are still in the world! We have jobs, businesses, homes, families, etc. We have full and abundant lives here, and we are connected to an eternal world that extends far beyond our physical world.

Understanding how to live in God's kingdom is an ongoing process. No sane person would expect a toddler to master college level courses. We expect him or her to learn to walk. In the same way, God knows what He expects from His children at each stage of their life. He is a loving and caring father, not a cruel taskmaster. He wants to build you up, not tear you down. He has work for you to do, and like any father, He wants His children to be prepared. He has invested enormous resources to see that His children have every opportunity to take root, sprout up, and grow.

Finding Your Way in the Kingdom of God

It is Knowledge that enables us to grow. If you want to find a specific restaurant in Dallas, you would not ask people in Milwaukee for directions. You would read a map of Dallas and ask people already living in Dallas for directions. In order to get help, you must know two critical pieces of information. You must know where you are now and where you want to go. Many people are lost and cannot get help, because they do not know where they are and where they want to go. Jesus said He came to seek and save the lost. You have help.

Let us say, you decide that you really want to find that restaurant in Dallas. You have heard so many good things about it, and you have been planning to go there for a long time. You are determined to get there and you say to yourself no matter what I am going. I have a general direction of where I think it is, and I am going to get in my car and try to find it.

After a while, it seems that you have been driving for a long time and things are starting to look unfamiliar. You stop and get directions and find that you have gone twenty miles in the wrong direction. You are frustrated and want to give up, but the thought of good food keeps running through your mind.

You decide to swallow your pride, admit you have made a mistake, and turn around. Finally, you get close to the area, but you still cannot find the restaurant. You check your directions and retrace your path in your head. You are confident that you followed the right directions this time, but you are still lost. Despair starts to set in. You are tired, hungry, and lost.

Finally, you pull over again and ask for directions. You stop someone and tell him the address you are trying to get to, and you are told you are only one block away. Just keep driving straight ahead one more block and you will be there. You are excited again; you hop back in the car with confidence and drive on. You get to the right address, but it does not look like a restaurant. You park, get out of the car, and look into the window. It is a flower shop not a restaurant.

You stop someone on the street and ask her where the restaurant is. She says you are at the right place, but the owner retired last month, sold the restaurant to the flower shop, and moved to Florida. Now, you are frustrated again. You finally got to the right place, but it was too late. If you had arrived a few weeks sooner, everything would have worked out fine. Perhaps, you were trying to find a new place based on outdated information.

This is life. Sometimes, you are right on point. You arrive at the right place at the right time on your first try. Other times, you do not. I want to encourage you not to give up. Nobody gets it right the first time, every time. Most of us get lost a few times. Sometimes we think we know the way, but we have gone a great distance in the wrong direction before we are humbled enough to ask for help.

Sometimes we are too late, the seasons have changed, and the opportunities have passed. Sometimes, we need to update our information before we set off on a journey. **If you study your methods, you can figure out where you went wrong.** Then develop a new plan and get going again. You will find another good restaurant, and you will eat until you are full. Remember there is abundance in the kingdom of God, not lack.

If you want to continue to grow in the kingdom of God, you need more knowledge. You must read the bible and ask people in the kingdom for guidance and direction. If you want to have a successful business in the kingdom of God, you need supernatural and natural knowledge. The supernatural knowledge provides wisdom and insight while natural knowledge provides the sound business skills you will need to succeed.

ADVANCING THE KINGDOM OF GOD

For far too long, the body of Christ has accepted the point of view that the responsibility for advancing the kingdom of God belongs to the clergy. At best, we were doing a good enough job to go to church on Sunday. The fired up Christians even went a step further and brought someone with them to church. **Overtime a subtle but pervasive view took hold that the kingdom of God was contained inside the church building.** God was at church. Satan ruled everywhere else. Every time Christians left the safe haven of the church building, they were walking into hostile enemy territory. After getting spiritually beat up all week long, they went back to the church on Sunday morning to get renewed and refreshed.

I thank God for the mighty men and women of God who have served in the capacity of clergy and advanced the kingdom of God. Many of us would not have survived had it not been for them. However, it was never God's intention for the clergy to bear the whole responsibility for advancing the kingdom. It is time for the rest of the body of believers to get to work and claim territory in the kingdom. People will listen if we tell them. They will wake up. They will build their lives according to the kingdom of God instead of the systems of this world. The whole earth belongs to our God.

Jesus said in Matthew 28:18,

> *all power is given unto me in heaven and in earth.*

Deuteronomy 1:21 says,

> *behold, the Lord thy God hath set the land before thee: go up and possess it, as the Lord God of thy fathers hath said unto thee; fear not, neither be discouraged.*

We are called to advance the kingdom of God through all areas of our lives, *a world without end, amen.* Entrepreneurs are able to build the kingdom of God by understanding how business and money works and applying these principles to everyday life. However, we are not the only builders. We are one part of the great body of Christ. We have an assignment to go up and take possession of the land through business ownership. We seek and rely on God's infinite knowledge, love, and wisdom to guide our path. **We stand face to face with the kings of this world and challenge them for the territory that belongs to our God, the king of kings.**

Hosea 4:6 tells us that people are destroyed for a lack of knowledge. More specifically today, people are destroyed for a lack of Godly knowledge, which they cannot access and apply to their everyday lives. This is not to condemn anyone. It simply to say you must continue to wake up, grow, and learn to get through the next phase of your life.

The whosoever will let them come and grow. The Word of God will not return void. The Holy Spirit will help us understand God's plan to bring each of us to our expected end. Some will become better readers, writers, and thinkers as they search the scriptures and discover the wisdom of God. Some will develop boldness as they present themselves to the world and claim the promises of God. Others will establish their own businesses or rise to the top of existing organizations and be witnesses for the kingdom of God. Along the way, we will all have our own personal encounters with Christ.

MY FOUNDATION

I remember the day my father told us that our mother had died. I had two older sisters and a younger brother. I was four years old. He was in his bed alone. He looked so sad. We asked him where is mama? After a while, he said she is gone to heaven. I remember asking when is she coming back. He said she is not coming back. She is gone. She has died. I did not understand what that meant. I remember going to the funeral and seeing her in the coffin. I just thought she was asleep. I remember taking a train ride from Milwaukee to North Carolina to bury her in her hometown. I do not remember feeling sad. I kept asking people when is she coming back, and they kept telling me she went to be with the angels in heaven. They described heaven to me, and I thought it must be a nice place. I liked to hear stories about heaven, because that was where mama was.

When I was seven years old, I ripped my dress at school while I was playing. A teacher said, in a mean way, what kind of mother would let you leave home without a slip. (I guess daddy did not know that little girls were supposed to wear slips under their dresses.) I said, I do not have a mama and I started to cry. They took me to the nurse's office. While the nurse was sewing my dress, she asked me questions about my mama. I told her that daddy said she was too was sick for the doctors to take of so the angels took her to heaven so Jesus could take care of her. I said I wanted to know how she was doing, but I did not know how to get to heaven. She told me that if I could get alone with God I could ask Him all the questions I wanted to about heaven and mama. I could ask Jesus to come into my heart and He would be my friend. She said I could talk to Him anytime I wanted to, and He could check on mama for me.

When I got home from school, I went into the bathroom, locked the door so I could be alone, and asked Jesus to come into my heart and be my friend. I felt His presence and mama's too. People told me that my mother was a saint and I asked Jesus if I could be one too. Over the years, I still kept waiting for mama to come back, but I did not feel that she was ever that far away. I felt that whenever I was in trouble, or afraid, or just needed direction I could just ask mama and Jesus for help. I felt loved and somehow shielded.

I grew up feeling as if I was living in two different worlds. I did not understand about the kingdom of God, until many years later but I experienced it long before I could explain it. I knew it was just as real as the physical world. As I got older, I tried to tell other people, but they acted as if I was just being childish and believing in make believe. Sometimes I thought I was, but mostly I just thought they were afraid to talk about God. In the same way that people are afraid to talk about death. Particularly, religious people who have a form of godliness but deny the power and nearness of God.

Some adults told me that no one could be born again at seven years old. They said a person has to be at least twelve years old to understand the seriousness of the decision. Some even said sixteen. Jesus said to let the little children come to Him.

Mark 10:13-16 says:

Then they brought little children to Him, that He might touch them; but the disciples rebuked those who brought them.

But when Jesus saw it, He was greatly displeased and said to them, Let the little children come to Me, and do not forbid them; for of such is the kingdom of God.

Assuredly, I say to you, whoever does not receive the kingdom of God as a little child will by no means enter it.

And He took them up in His arms, laid His hands on them, and blessed them.

Evangelism researchers tell us that eighty percent of Christians received Christ before the age of twenty. When I came to Jesus, I did not need anyone to go through the bible with me and show me scripture after scripture of why I should believe. I did not need Jesus to be on trial and make a decision as a judge does in a court case. He did not need a defense attorney or a prosecutor. All I needed to know was that mama was with Him. I loved my mama, and I knew that she loved me. I was happy to know that she was with Jesus. If He was good enough to take care of her, I knew He would take of me.

We use time to gauge things, but time is different in the kingdom of God. Sometimes we asked people how long they have been a Christian to determine at what level they are. Only God determines that. There is no timeframe for levels. Jesus was teaching in the synagogue at twelve, and He is our precept and example. Many children understand a great deal more about the kingdom of God than adults think they do.

Many children have lost parents through death, divorce, or abandonment. I speak peace and restoration into your soul right now. I want to encourage anyone who has an unfulfilled need or a pain that tugs at his or her soul. If God can comfort a little girl that lost her mama, and give her the peace that passes all understanding, He can heal the inner most parts of your life.

It is the power of God that calls to us regardless of age. He calls to seven-year-olds and he calls to seventy-seven-year-olds and everyone in between. He calls us to come and meet at His throne of grace to begin a new life that will never end.

> *But as many as received Him, to them He gave the right to become children of God, even to those who believe in His name, John 1:12.*

He, who has an ear to hear, let him hear what the spirit is saying. We are not alone. We are in the company of saints. We are a part of the kingdom of God. The veil was ripped for all of us to come personally to Him whether from an altar, a bathroom, a ballroom, a prison, a classroom, a hospital, an executive boardroom, or a car. The spirit of God is alive and it lives within us. The kingdom of God manifested in earthen vessels cutting across space, time, culture, religion, occupation, nationality, race, gender, social status, and age.

In addition, Jesus did not come to set up a church building or choose one church building over another. He did not come to set up denominations or choose one denomination over the other. People do that. God is not against that, though. He divided the children of Israel into tribes and separated their territories. However, He did establish certain times for all of them to come together. Therefore, he expects us to go beyond our tribes at appointed times and come together as one body. Jesus is the head of the body, and He is moved when we have a personal encounter with Him. Then, we are free to attend any house of worship we choose as long as our main house of worship is within us, God in us.

THE STORY OF JOSEPH

Let us study the life of Joseph, from Genesis 37-48. Joseph was the favored son of his father Jacob. He was the 11th of 12 sons. **Joseph had two dreams**. In the first, his brothers would one day bow down to him and serve him. In the second, his parents would also bow down to him. Joseph's brothers did not receive this well and plotted to kill him. His brother Rueben convinced them not to kill him but to put him in a pit in the wilderness. Rueben had planned to come back later and rescue him. In the meantime, the other brothers got him out of the pit and sold him to a caravan going to Egypt. Joseph wound up as a slave serving in the house of Potiphar, who was captain of the guard, an officer of Pharoah.

Joseph served with such excellence that Potiphar put him in charge of his entire household. Things had been bad for Joseph but now they were looking up. until Potiphar's wife lied and claimed that Joseph tried to seduce her. Potiphar put Joseph in jail. Things were looking bad for Joseph again. He served in the prison with such excellence, that the warden put him in charge of all the prisoners. Things were getting a little better for him. Pharaoh's baker and cupbearer, who were also in prison, had dreams one day. **Joseph correctly interpreted their dreams.** The cupbearer was released from prison and restored to his former position with pharaoh. Joseph asked the cupbearer to remember him before pharaoh so that he too could be released from prison. The cupbearer forgot.

Two years later, Pharaoh had two dreams that no one could interpret. The cupbearer remembered Joseph. Pharaoh summoned Joseph out of prison and **Joseph correctly interpreted Pharaoh's dreams**. Joseph told Pharaoh that there would be seven years of abundance for Egypt followed by seven years of famine. He told him that he should appoint a wise man to administrate the business affairs of the nation to ensure that during the years of famine enough would be stored up and the nation would survive. Pharaoh chose Joseph. He took him out of prison for good and made him second to him in charge of the whole nation.

Proverbs 22:29 says, do you see a man diligent in his business? He shall stand before kings; he shall not stand before obscure men. Joseph developed a business plan. During the seven years of abundance, he collected 20% of the food produced and stored it up in the nearby cities. When the famine came, he sold the food back to the people. Notice, he sold it not gave it. When the people ran out of money, they traded their livestock for food, then their land, then their labor. The one with the plan succeeded and the one without became his servant in order to survive.

Joseph saved his entire family from starvation and he did rule over them. The dream he had twenty years earlier did materialize. Sometimes people will mock your dream and even try to destroy you. You must hold on to the dream that God has given you. He will build into you whatever you need to bring that dream to fruition.

Key Points to Remember

- Owning a business is valuable equity building investment that can pass from generation to generation if built on a solid foundation
- Hearing and *doing* what the word of God says is the foundation that enables us to stand the storms of life
- Jesus gives us the power to become
- The systems of this world operate out of scarcity and competition
- The kingdom of God operates out of abundance not lack
- Entry into the kingdom of God is only through Jesus
- The kingdom of God enters us and we enter it
- The kingdom of God is alive and flourishing

- We need supernatural and natural knowledge in order to grow
- The entire body of Christ is commissioned to advance the kingdom of God in every area of life
- Entrepreneurs are called to claim territory in the kingdom of God through business ownership
- God calls us according to His time frame not ours
- 80% of Christians receive Christ before the age of twenty
- The kingdom of God must be received by faith like that of a child
- Joseph endured many hardships before his dream came to fruition
- As in the case of Joseph, God blesses us so we can be a blessing to others

Notes

2

The Planning Process

But seek ye first the kingdom of God,
and his righteousness;

and all these things shall be added unto you.

Matthew 6:33

Who Can Be an Entrepreneur?

Entrepreneurs establish and lead businesses including churches and ministries. Entrepreneurs are visionaries. They are people who see an opportunity that they are uniquely suited for, and are willing to pursue it. It takes faith, a great deal of hard work, the ability to relate and sell to others, and above all integrity. **Christian entrepreneurs are gifted and called by God to serve the body of Christ, through the creation of jobs, goods, and services.**

We all come from different walks of life. The Holy Spirit imparts to us different spiritual gifts. Therefore, we will experience God differently. He will speak specifically to you in a language you understand. He will guide you according to the gifts He has placed in you. Our God is a creator. He made us in His image, and we are creative. He provides His children with supernatural insight to give us an advantage over other people. That means that as an entrepreneur, you will be able to look at a product, service, or situation and see an opportunity that others cannot see. It is your God given right and responsibility to pursue it and claim the promises of God.

There are some books written by *experts* that describe the characteristics of entrepreneurs. They divide them into neat categories and say that successful entrepreneurs have these or those characteristics. The implication is that in order for you to succeed you must have similar characteristics. Out of the billions of people on the planet, it is impossible to fit all of them into a few man made categories. It is much more important that you believe you are a child of God operating in the kingdom of God rather than the compilation of characteristics. God is in the business of setting us free from the restrictions that have bound us in the past. You are who God says you are, and you can do what God says you can do.

Since we are still in the world but no longer of this world, some of the principles we learned in this world are still valid in the kingdom of God. Jesus said we should be shrewd and work these principles to our benefit. We will fuse together what we need for where we are going. This world belongs to our God, and we intend to rise up and take hold of everything that God has put at our disposal.

Business and business opportunities are happening all around us. Someone created and sold most of the things you touch in the course of a day. First, there is a thought or idea. Then a product produced, sold to wholesaler, sold to a retailer, and then sold to you. Somewhere along that chain, there is an opportunity waiting for you to capitalize on it. However, you cannot sit back and wait around for opportunities to drop in your lap. Your life will pass you by. Faith without works is dead. You must actively in engage in life. *The kingdom of heaven suffereth violence and the violent take it by force,* Matthew 11:12.

Knowledge of who you are and what you are created to be is a powerful weapon. There is a saying that most people have thought up good business ideas in the shower. Entrepreneurs get out of the shower and put those ideas to work. Others simply get out of the shower. Today is the day you begin to put those ideas to work. They will work for you. You can be an entrepreneur. All of creation is waiting to see what you will become.

CAN YOUR BUSINESS SUCCEED?

We have all heard the threatening statistics that at least 70% of new business start-ups fail within the first year, and over half of all new churches fail within the first three years and far fewer ever attract a sizeable congregation. If we take a closer look at the statistics for very small businesses, we see an entirely different picture. The five-year survival rate for one person establishments is 61%; 70% for two to three person establishments; and 75% for four to seven person establishments according to the Small Business Administration (SBA) research published in December 2006. This tells us that with the right foundation and the right opportunity, most entrepreneurs will succeed. However, the storms of life will still come. Therefore, you have to be wise and count on them and plan for them.

We will go through the process of what it really takes to start and run an actual business. We will decide on a product, design, purchase, and sell it. We will develop a business plan, budget, market, sell, produce financial reports, pay overhead expenses, and set goals for the next venture. We will emphasize the reality of starting a small business. You start where you are, but look to where you are going. Too many people never start, because they feel they do not have enough. God provides us with power and courage. Most very small businesses are originally started with a few saved and a few borrowed dollars. **We need knowledge in order to grow.** We will focus on how to keep expenses low, develop good people and business skills, perseverance, and planning. God has the ultimate responsibility for the outcome.

Business encompasses almost every aspect of our lives. It is not surprising why the word of God is full of so many lessons about it. We will study the word of God to see how God raised up ordinary people to do extraordinary things. The Bible tells us that we are to do business until Jesus returns. He should find us busy, actively working. Aggressively gaining territory until, the kingdoms of this world become the kingdoms of our God.

THE BUSINESS PLAN

Definition

A business plan is a summary of how a business or entrepreneur intends to organize an entrepreneurial endeavor and implement activities necessary and sufficient for the venture to succeed. It is a written explanation of the company's business model for the venture in question.

Business plans come in all shapes and sizes. There are some general templates to use, if you are writing one to obtain a loan or some other kind of funding. Since we are not, we will use a plan that is relevant and useful to the business we want to start. First, we will use a simple wholesale/retail model that involves selecting a product and selling to the public.

Wholesalers sell products in large quantities at lower prices to retailers. Retailers sell the products in smaller quantities and higher prices directly to the consumer. For example if a consumer wants to buy one T-shirt, he cannot buy directly from the wholesaler. The wholesaler may only sell T-shirts by the hundreds.

- The retailer will buy one hundred T-shirts for $5.00 each or $500.
- He will then sell the individual T-shirts for $10 each, a $5.00 or 100% markup per T-shirt.
- If he can sell them all, he makes $1000, $10 x 100 T-shirts= $1000.
- The $500 difference is his profit.
- If he cannot sell them all, he must sell at least half to break even, $10 x 50 T-shirts = $500.
- Retailers must adjust their prices and their profit margin according to how well a product is selling.

In addition to paying for the cost of the product, the business owner must also pay overhead expenses. They include rent, utilities, wages, taxes, insurance, advertising, store displays, maintenance, professional advisors fees, trade association fees, etc. He must be aware of his competition and sensitive to the needs of his customers. To be successful, he must develop his spiritual ears to hear the voice of God guiding him. Matthew 13:9 says *who hath ears to hear, let him hear*. It will tell him when to make a move in a direction and when to pass. Knowledge and experience develops sensitivity to and faith in that voice.

Financial Goal

For the purpose of this example,

- We will start with a budget of $500.
- Our goal is to produce $1000 of gross income and at least a $500 profit.
- If you do not have $500, you can start with $50. The process is the same.

- We will keep our overhead expenses low in order to maximize our profits.

If you build your business slowly and methodically, you will have time to learn about all the overhead expenses as they come along. They should come as a natural growing progression of your business.

A common mistake that new entrepreneurs make is having too much money go out and not enough to come in, top heavy. There is common misconception that you do not have a real business until you have a retail space, and that having a retail space is going to help you make more money. This is not true. Before you sign a multi year lease and pay the property owner thousands of dollars, you should have your business up and running. We will talk more about that in chapter 6.

Most small businesses start at home. In a wholesale/retail business, it is usually not desirable to sell directly from your home. There are low cost alternatives. The type of product you select, will naturally lend itself to certain environments. Your budget and financial goals will be other determining factors.

Product/Idea Generation

We will select a business that will be short term, but one that can easily be developed into an ongoing business. This is how you will test a product or market before investing a lot of money in it. It is also how you make money to build your business. A well-known product type should sell quickly with at least a 100% mark-up. Since you do not have a retail space, it needs to be lightweight, portable, and able to appeal to a wide range of customers.

I want to be careful not to plant a specific idea. It is important that you trust God to guide you. If you ask Him, He will answer. Look at a product or opportunity that appeals to you, and ask God is this the one for me? You can ask Him more questions. Where shall I sell it, for how much, for how long, to what people, why would they buy it from me? If you truly ask him and wait for an answer, you will be surprised. He will answer. He will order your steps and lead you to products and services for you to sell.

He will give you supernatural insight, and you will select products and services that agree with your spirit.

When God says yes, things will line up in order. Doors open to us. He gives to us according to our faith. When we go ahead of God, things are hard. We struggle in an uphill battle. We begin to sense that we are operating in our own strength instead of the power of God. We must back up, retrace our steps to the place where we left Him, and start listening again to His voice.

The following are general guidelines to help you start searching for your products.

- The product should not cost a lot or need much explanation to sell. In a mobile environment, people are usually willing to spend $5 to $10 quickly, particularly if the product is known but unique enough not to sell everywhere.
- You should sell at round numbers, and for security, you may want to make change as seldom as possible. For example, you want to sell 100 items at $10 each or 200 items at $5 each.
- You can start searching for your product by searching the web for wholesalers who meet the criteria. Most publish extensive catalogs with their product offerings. Most large cities have wholesale districts that you can visit.
- You will be looking for products sold at wholesale for under $5.00, that you can resale for $10.00. If you have to pay for shipping and handling, you will have to go lower to $4.00 or $4.50. If you want to sell some $5.00 items, you will need to buy items at $2.00 or $2.50.
- The wholesaler may require you to order items by the hundreds, dozens, or gross. A gross is twelve dozen.
- It is a good idea to select several products. One product will be your lead product then choose a couple more that support it. This will give your customers options and help broaden your appeal.

The product you select should be appropriate to the setting where you will be selling. You must also be the appropriate person to sell it. Some products are gender specific. Some require a certain amount of knowledge about a trade or hobby. Some products sell very well in one region of the country and not at all in other regions. This can even be true in certain parts of the same city. Some products are seasonal, and it is important to time your product to arrive in the right season.

Some products sell primarily from a catalog. However, this is usually just for friends and family. Most people, that do not know you, do not want to place an order and wait for it, unless it is a customized product. If you want to expand, you are going to have to buy inventory. If possible, select products that people would normally buy for themselves. That way, you are helping them stay within their budget.

Marketplace

Marketing, in its simplest form, is a process of getting sellers and buyers together at a marketplace. A marketplace is a location where the exchange of goods and services takes place. Marketplaces are everywhere, but you do not necessarily see them until you begin to look for them. It is time to begin to look. You should begin to look for marketplaces through the eyes of a business owner. You will need to find a place where your potential buyers are likely to gather or pass through.

Most communities have some type of marketplace where you can pay a small vendor fee to sell your merchandise. An example of this would be, renting a booth at a local Fourth of July celebration, or at a convention, or kiosk at the local mall. Of course, the bigger the event the more it will cost to rent the space, but people generally come to these places expecting to spend money. You can also choose a location where people gather or travel through and simply approach them. This is often very productive and helps you to learn effective selling techniques.

In centuries past, the traveling salesman would put his wares on his horse drawn wagon and go door to door to sell his products. The marketplace was the front door. In some regions of the country, this is still a popular marketplace. Today, we can even go beyond the door via the television, Internet, and radio. Television and radio are usually too expensive for new startup companies. However, the Internet is a low cost alternative. Internet marketplaces such as websites and eBay are worth considering as you build your business.

You should look at businesses in your community through the eyes of a business owner. Can you appreciate the time, planning, hard work, and courage it must have taken to build that business? Every one of them had an initial start up phase. You would probably be surprised to know that many of them started by doing some of the same things that you will do to begin your business. The next time you see a vendor at a community event walk over and encourage them, buy something. **This is one your fellow entrepreneurs who stepped out of his comfort zone to make his dreams a reality.**

Starting a Wholesale/Retail Business

Name Selection

We will move from the classroom, to the field to start a business. First, we need to name our business. We need a name that reflects us and is broad enough to grow in several different directions as our business grows. **Since we are building the kingdom of God, we will call our business Kingdom of God Builders.** Next, we go to the county courthouse and make sure that there is not a business already registered in our county with that name. If not, we pay a small fee and officially register it as a sole proprietorship. The clerk will give us a certificate and we are on our way to starting a business. You will need this certificate to open a business bank account, apply for tax identification number and for other business uses that we will talk more about in later chapters. To apply for tax identification number, we simply go to the IRS website and follow the instructions. This is free.

Marketplace Selection

For the purpose of this example, we will decide to be a vendor. We begin by searching for a marketplace. We can start by looking throughout our community. We can also search the Internet for places within our local community, which we might not be aware. You can type in the name of your city, then community events or something similar to that. Then, narrow down the list by dates.

Let us say you find that there will be a community festival this summer, and you have a couple months to prepare. **The website gives a lot of information that is helpful**. The expected attendance is around five thousand people; a family oriented event that takes place every summer. There will be rides, games, food, music, and other activities going on throughout the day. It mentions that vendors are welcome and gives sign up information. The booth prices range from $50 to $125. You can sign up online or in person. The contact information is given.

You continue to look online and make notes of a few other events. Somehow, they do not seem quite as appealing as this one. **Before you sign up though, it is a good idea to go in person and look at the site.** This gives information that you cannot get by just reading about a place. Look at several sites and make notes of what you see and feel. You can get a feel for the size of the area and the likely arrangement of things. It should be clean and inviting. Your spirit should connect with the overall atmosphere.

You should visit the sign up office in person and ask some questions. Such as, what determines the price of the booths? The organizers can usually show you a map of the booth arrangements. It is important to know where other things will be such as the food stands. Where will people enter and exit the festival? Will there be a main stage? It is important to get a feel for how the foot traffic will flow. **You want to make sure you position yourself in a high traffic area.** Usually, the spaces between the main stage and food court are high traffic areas. Entrances and exits are also good places. These are usually the higher priced booths, and they are well worth it. Since you will be outside in the sun and heat, you want to know if the organizers provide canopies. If not, are you free to bring your own covering?

After reviewing the map, you determine that there is a good space available on a path between the food court and the main stage. The organizers will provide canopies, and that booth is $100. This is a good time to stop and pray. Everything looks good. The price is right. **Can you feel that God is bringing things in line for you?** Do you feel a sense of calmness in your spirit? You can walk around the park. Pray and ask God is this it? Is this the place you want me to begin my business? If you pause in your spirit and wait for answer, He will answer you.

If you feel that He said yes, you should go ahead and rent the space. If you feel that He definitely said no, you must look somewhere else. If you are not sure, you should take a day or two and continue to pray, meditate on the Word of God, and consider other options. If everything seems to keep leading you back to that place, then God is probably leading you to that spot. It may be your own fears rising up as doubt. You have to step out on faith. For the purpose of our example, we rent the booth for $100. They give us a receipt and a confirmation. We need to keep all of our receipts for our financial records.

Product selection

After choosing our location, we need to find products to sell. Since we will be outside in a park and in a family oriented setting, we should choose appropriate products. **We will choose one primary and two secondary products in order to appeal to a broader range of customers than just one product.** We look at wholesalers' catalogs for ideas and make a list of possibilities that meet our criteria. For this example, we choose T-shirts to be our primary product. Sunglasses and water squirt gun toys will be our secondary products.

First, we will develop our primary product. T-shirts are already a well-known product that is able to appeal to a wide range of customers. We need to come up with a design or slogan to distinguish our T-shirts. Most

T-shirt companies have catalogs or online design programs to help us with this. They also help us determine how much it will cost for our design. After experimenting with several different options, we come up with a good design at a good price. Our wholesaler offers free shipping which will allow us to order more t-shirts. The final price will be $4.00 per t-shirt. We can sell them at retail for $10.00 each.

We will use a white T-shirt because it has a broad appeal and white is a lower cost than color T-shirts. **Our slogan will be, *To God be the Glory*.** Our slogan is evangelistic in nature and is consistent with our theme of keeping God at the center of all we do. We will write our slogan across the front with blue letters. We chose blue letters, because blue will match many colors and clothes including blue jeans.

Next, we determine the sizes we will need. Again, the t-shirt company can help us with this. We tell them a brief description of our event, how many t-shirts we want to order, and how much we want to spend. We can use their expertise to suggest the most popular sizes. We come up with the following summary of our primary product:

T-shirt summary

- T-shirts with the slogan To God be the Glory
- Style: White T-shirt, blue lettering
- Quantity and Sizes: 2XL-15, XL-20, L-10, SM-15
- Wholesale Price: $4 per shirt x 60 shirts= $240
- Retail Price: $10 per shirt x 60 shirts= $600

Now, we develop our next product, sunglasses. We **chose sunglasses, because our event will be outside in a park.** We expect the weather to be warm and sunny. We make this a secondary product because if it turns out to be a cloudy day it will affect our sells. We begin our search for sunglasses with online wholesalers. After searching around and comparing styles and prices, we come up with a selection. The wholesaler offers a recommended package of bestsellers that meets our budget. We can buy fifty pairs of sunglasses for $2.00 each, and they provide free shipping. We will sell them at retail for $5.00 each.

Sunglasses summary:

- Style: variety of styles for men and women recommended by the wholesaler as bestsellers
- Quantity: 50
- Wholesale price: $2 each x 50= $100
- Retail Price: $5 each x 50= $250

Our next product is something to keep the kids entertained. It needs to be appropriate to our park setting on a warm summer day. We search our wholesale catalogs. We find squirt guns/water blasters that are in a bright eye-catching package. They cost $1.00 each. This wholesaler does not offer free shipping. We get a quote, and it will cost $10 to have them shipped to us. Therefore, we can spend $50. These toys are very appealing and we decide to sell them for $3.00 each.

Kids water toys summary:

- Style: squirt guns/water blasters
- Quantity: 50
- Wholesale price: $1 each x 50 = $50
- Shipping cost: $10.00
- Retail price: $3 each x 50= $150

Total to spend: $240 + $100 + $60 = $400 + $100 booth rent = $500
Expected income if all products are sold: $600 + $250 +150 = $1000

If you do not have the $500 that we used in the example and you only have $50, you can simply start with a dollar item, such as the toys. You will not need to rent a booth. You can sell to your friends, family, neighbors, and coworkers. You can work your way up to buying and selling more items. Everything else about building a business still applies to you simply correct the figures. You can be an entrepreneur. If you trust God, He will take your seed and bless it.

In Mark 4:30-32 Jesus said,

> *Whereunto shall we liken the kingdom of God? Or with what comparison shall we compare it?*
>
> *It is like a grain of mustard seed, which, when it is sown in the earth, is less than all the seeds that be in the earth:*
>
> *But when it is sown, it groweth up, and becomes greater that all herbs, and shooteth out great branches; so that the fowls of the air may lodge under the shadow of it.*

In the kingdom of God, a little seed sown in faith produces great results. Our God is awesome!

STARTING A SERVICE BUSINESS

Service business plans are similar to the wholesale/retail model. Instead of buying a product to sell, **you sell your service or expert knowledge in a field**. Your start up expenses comes from developing a marketing package and from acquiring the tools of the trade. If your business will be one where you travel to your customers' sites or use the internet, you have the advantage of working out of your home for years. I know a Christian plumber who has done this for fifteen years. He has an ad in the yellow pages and on the Internet, an answering service, a phone, a truck, and two employees. He makes a lot of money and keeps his overhead low.

I also know an accountant that works from home. He has clients all over the country as an independent auditor for corporations. He does most of his business over the internet. He travels to a company only when he needs to make a presentation and charges them for his traveling expenses. He has enough time to serve as an associate pastor of a church.

Some of the most precious benefits of owning your own business are the freedom to structure your time, work environment, and lifestyle.

Do you have an idea for a service or information business, but you do not know how to sell your services or even if anyone is willing to pay for them? We need to create a sample service business. Let us say you have a kind heart and have a gift for helping people in crisis. You already have specific credentials that qualify you to help people in this way. **You decide you want to be a grief counselor.** Specifically, you want to help families that have lost loved ones and do not seem to be coping. You want to work with them in their home environment and help them to move pass their grief. You need to identify some payment sources for your services. **Your product is your expertise in this area. You need a plan to help aim you in a specific direction.**

First, you will need to contact your state's licensing board and find out the criteria for a obtaining a license. Your state's department of health or human services can guide you to the right place. You will receive some sort of licensing packet with instructions you need to follow. If you do not possess the necessary qualifications, you need to make a plan for getting them. If you need to earn money while you work on getting qualified, you can still consider doing a wholesale/retail business. You can select products and marketplaces that relate to that field. This will bring you into contact with people who later may be instrumental to you as a grief counselor. You need to begin positioning yourself for where you are going.

You need to write out some actions steps, such as the following:

- Identify community resources that are already available and gaps in those services that you can fill
- Put a grieving program together to help people at different ages and stages of life
- Develop a pricing structure for your services by finding the prevailing rate for similar services

- Put together a marketing kit—letterheads, business cards, postcards, web site, email address, and brochures to introduce yourself and your services.
- Make a list of local funeral homes, hospitals, hospices, home health agencies, churches and doctors who come in contact with people who could benefit from your services, visit them periodically and ask for referrals
- Determine how similar services are already being paid and how your service can be paid for through similar channels
- Research sources for grants and write a proposal
- Write an article for the local newspaper or a magazine explaining why some people cope better with grief than others.
- Keep copies of the articles to help establish your credibility in this area
- Start a support group and charge a fee according to the participants ability to pay

This is a needed service in the community and in the kingdom of God. If you have a sincere heart and the ability to help people, God will step in and help you. He will guide you systematically. **Your gift will make room for you.** Your business will grow and you will affect the lives of many people. This compassionate business will touch the very heart of God. You will be a point of light positioned to lead souls to the kingdom.

OVERCOMING FEAR

The learning experience during this early stage is invaluable. Every business owner must know how to plan and sell. It is the basis of all business. The people that learn how to do this will excel financially in any field. **Planning enables you to overcome fear, approach strangers, present yourself and/or your product, make the sale, and become prosperous. This is a foundational principle to gaining territory in the kingdom of God.**

You will need the support of at least one other person. You must find someone you can count on for advice and encouragement. There will be times when you need someone to talk things over. You need someone to celebrate with you when times are good, and someone to encourage you when times are hard. *Deuteronomy 32:30 says, one can chase a thousand and two can put ten thousand to flight.* If you do not have anyone, you can ask God to direct your steps. He will lead you to someone. You will be confident, because you will know that you are on a mission. God will use every interaction to teach valuable lessons to help you grow.

He is in the process of raising you up to lead your corporation, church and perhaps a whole nation just as Joseph did. The journey of a thousand miles begins with the first step. The battle begins in our minds with I cannot, and ends in our actions with amazement of what God has gifted us to be able to do. **We begin to break the bondage of fear right now,** casting down fearful imaginations, and everything that exalts itself above the knowledge of what God has already determined for our lives.

Nothing that you have is as important as what God wants to give you. He has given entrepreneurs the desire to create wealth and help people. He wants to see His children prosperous and free. He is concerned about our material success. Not so we can hoard it, worship it or parade it over others, but so that we can enjoy it. Business owners and investors also establish and contribute more to charities, philanthropic, and religious organizations than any other group of people. **If you desire to be a blessing to people, you need the financial means to be able to help them.** Your faith, knowledge, and right action overcome fear.

Key Points to Remember

- Christian entrepreneurs are gifted and called by God
- Most entrepreneurial pursuits will succeed
- A business plan should be relevant and useful
- Pray and ask God to open your eyes, ears, and mind to all the possibilities that are within your reach
- Follow God's lead

- As you go through your day, ask Him is there an opportunity for me here?
- Set a financial goal
- Select a name, product, and marketplace that agrees with your spirit
- In a service business your service and/or expertise is your product
- Faith, knowledge, and right action overcome fear

Notes

3

Time to Sell

But seek ye first the kingdom of God,
and his righteousness;

and all these things shall be added unto you.

Matthew 6:33

LEARNING TO SELL

This is the most exciting stage of all. Once you have selected your product, determined where and when to sell, it is time for all of the planning to pay off. You move from talking the talk to walking the walk. **You do not have a business unless you can sell your product or service**.

Key points:

- Believe in yourself
- Believe that God has not brought you this far to leave you
- Believe that what you have to sell is a valuable commodity that people want
- Write out a sales pitch and practice it
- See yourself talking to people and making sales
- Anticipate questions that customers are likely to ask and prepare answers
- Practice role playing with your partner or friends
- Pre-sell to a friendly crowd to test your skills
- Expect the unexpected and have a back-up plan
- Stay upbeat and positive
- Do your homework
- Study the competition
- Study your product
- Study your potential customers
- At first, more sales are lost than won

The art of selling is learned. People are not naturally born with the ability to sell. Even though good salespeople make it appear this way. Most salespeople spend a lot of time preparing. Do not worry about rejection, listen to what people say, and make adjustments if you feel you need to and keep moving. If you talk to ten people and give up, how do you know whether or not eleven through twenty would have bought enough to make up for the ten that did not?

Some people are great at presenting their product but fail at closing the sale. **The key is that you present your product, give the price, ask for the sale, and then be quiet. The person who speaks next loses**. You do not want to talk yourself out of a sale. If the customer says no, bless them and move on. Never harass people, and do not beg. You have a secret weapon. The Holy Spirit will intercede for you. Whisper a quick prayer and invite Him to go before you and prepare your way. He will. **Christian entrepreneurs are great at closing the sale. It is a gift from God**. We just have to practice it to activate it. He will usually start you small and over time raise you up to close bigger and bigger deals.

In the beginning, you will not have money for an advertising campaign; you can take advantage of the advertising done by the big companies. Simply reference it. For instance by saying, this product is something like this or that. Compare and contrast your product to a well-known one. Just make it clear that it is not that product. It is never worth it to lie or cheat people. Do not make negative remarks about other companies or products. Do not say your product is better than theirs is. If you have to do a lot of explaining, then your product is too complicated for this beginning phase. The time for selling high end or complex products will come, but if you are broke, you do not have the money to invest in them right now. The bible says despise not the days of small beginnings.

You will be able to sell. I speak peace and prosperity into your spirit right now. You will make money. You will make a lot of money. I have seen it done repeatedly. The problem is not making the money. It is managing it and all that comes with it. You must ground yourself in the word of God to be truly successful in all areas of your life.

PROVIDE GOOD CUSTOMER SERVICE

You have to believe in the product or service you are selling to build a successful business. Anybody can sell junk to people they do not care about, but they will not build a successful business. They are building their business upon the sand, when the storms come, it will not stand. We are not just building a business we are building in the kingdom of God with His permission and guidance. One day, we want to hear Him say, well-done good and faithful servant well done. There is absolutely no way to do this without communicating with Him every step of the way.

God will send customers to you. You will be searching for them, and they will be searching for you. When you find each other, be as gracious and sincere as you can. If you care about them and their needs, they will send other customers to you. **Satisfied customers will do your best marketing.** Never put profits before people. Sometimes there will be people that genuinely cannot benefit from your product, do not sell to them. There will be times when your competition has exactly what your customer needs and you do not. You must refer them. God *will* supply your needs. As much as humanly possible, do not worry.

You must be reliable. You are responsible for making yourself available. If you say, you are going to be at a certain place at a certain time, be there, and have your products available. Do not expect the customer to hunt you down. Study the market and know at what price others are selling the product. Price your product competitively. Do not hustle or cheat people. Do the opposite, go out of your way to find them good products and services at good prices. Do not ask people to do business with you out of obligation. You should expect them to do business with you, because you are offering them what they want at a good price, and you care about them. Put yourself in your customer's shoes. If I were they, wanted this product, and had the money to pay, would I buy it? Would I buy it from me? Why would I or why not?

People love to buy things that provide value to them, but they hate to be sold. Explain your product in terms of how it provides value to your customer. Sometimes this is obvious. For instance, if you are selling sunglasses on a hot and sunny day, you do not need to explain the value of sunglasses. The price, style, and competition are the variables. Explain why they should it buy it from you in terms of how it provides value to them. In other words, this style and color is attractive on you, and it only cost $5.00. This is speaking to the needs of customer. As opposed to saying, I am trying to start my own business and I want to sell my products. That is speaking to your need. It is not the customer's responsibility to be concerned about your needs. You want to understand theirs. You must be sincere.

You should try to sell customers several items. However if they only want to buy one, I never insult them by being pushy. I am honored they at least decided to buy one item from me. Sometimes, they even come back and bring someone else with them.

If you write the price down, the customer is more likely to trust you. Write it on the product or the display. They tend to think that you are making the price up as you go along if it is not in writing. It also taps into the visual sense. It confirms what you say to their hearing sense and touching taps into their tactile sense.

You should use positive words that are complimentary but not flirtatious. Likewise if the customer is flirtatious, you should keep directing their attention back to the products and speak with a professional tone. This is not gender specific. Men and women salespeople have to gauge when conversations become inappropriate and need to have a plan for moving the focus back to the business. **Sometimes people are inappropriate, because their motives are bad.** They are purposely trying to be a distraction. You cannot afford to get so caught up with them that you lose track of what is going on around you.

Your primary focus is on building your business and to that end claiming territory in the kingdom of God. When Jesus sent out the seventy-two workers into the harvest field, He said, "*Go! I am sending you out like lambs among wolves,*" Luke 10:3 NIV. He went on to give them instructions on how to conduct themselves. When they returned Jesus said, *"I saw Satan fall like lightning from heaven,"* Luke10:18 NIV. Verse 17 said the *seventy-two returned with joy*. As you go out under the instruction of the word of

God, you must remember you have an assignment. If you stick to the plan, you will see Satanic spirits fall and you will return with joy.

Kingdom of God Builders continued

We are going to continue with the retail business we started in the last chapter, Kingdom of God Builders. We have work to do to prepare for our event. First, we must place the order. We need to know how much time it will take the wholesaler to get our order to us. If we place it too late, it may arrive too late and we will not have anything to sell at our event. If we place it too far in advance, we tie up our money in inventory, which can cause a cash flow problem as our business grows.

Once we have contacted our wholesaler and determined that they need two weeks, we will place the order about three weeks before our event. Two weeks later, our order arrives. We need to check all of our products to make sure they are what we ordered and everything is in good order.

Next, we need to make the following inventory log listing exactly what we have.

Starting	Number Sold	Balance
T-shirts- quantities		
2XL 15		
1XL 20		
Large 10		
Small 15		
Sunglasses		
50 pairs		
Toys		
50		

We will complete our inventory log after we have sold our products. This inventory log will provide us with useful information. It will tell us what is selling and what is not. It helps us determine what items to reorder and in what quantities. For instance if small t-shirts are selling faster than 2XL, we need to make an adjustment and order more small and less 2XL next time. The inventory log will also help us track our money. The amount of money we made should match our inventory sold, after accounting for any items not sold due to damage and/or theft. As our business grows, we will need to find a computer program that will make this task simpler. Many retailers use barcodes to track their inventory and sales.

About a week before the event, we need to:

- Call the organizers and confirm that everything is still on track
- Know what time to arrive and where to park and unload
- Know what time the event will end and what, if any, special requirements there are for exiting.
- Plan how we will organize our products within our booth to make them appealing to customers.
- Make sure to go to the bank and get small bills for making change for our customers. It can be very frustrating to lose sells because there is no change.
- Consider how to keep money in a secure place. People will be roaming around throughout the event, and you cannot assume that everyone is honest.

Finally, the big day has arrived. You have prayed. You are well prepared and ready to sell. You set up your booth and everything looks good. The hardest part is over. People will walk around and visit the booths. If they stop, you can be friendly, smile, tell them about your products, answer questions, and ask them to buy. Some will and some will not but do not worry. You will do well. It should be a relaxed, fun environment. You should have fun while you run your business. I have done this many times; I wish I could go with you. Since I cannot, I will be with you in spirit. Pray and ask God to go before you and prepare your way. I will share with you some of my experiences in various types of businesses. I hope that you will learn from my successes and mistakes. I have.

My First Business

When I was 12 years old, I started a business selling candy at school. I bought suckers for a nickel and sold them for a dime. I brought one hundred suckers to school every day and always sold out. I earned about $10 and made a profit of $5 each day. That was $25/week. That is equivalent to at least $100/week these days. That was not bad for a twelve year old.

The same suckers that I sold for a dime sold in the stores for a nickel. The same kids complained everyday about having to pay a dime for what they could buy at the store for a nickel. My answer was always the same; go buy it at the store. They never did. **Every day they came to school and gave me their dimes for what they could have bought for themselves for a nickel**. I usually sold my suckers at lunch or after school. It took about twenty minutes to sell one hundred suckers. Most kids bought four or five at a time. I would stop by the store on the way home and buy more. I made my money being willing to do what my customers would not. They wanted the product and knew where to get it cheaper, but simply were not willing to plan. My price was fair. They paid for convenience.

Over the years, I have often wondered why some young people are involved in illegal activities to make money. There are ways to make legitimate money. Most young people will follow the public and private ways of the adults in their environment. We need to take care to train up children with a kingdom of God mentality. We need to show them what they can become and all they can have by believing in God. We need to show them not just tell them.

Selling Advertisements

The next experience that comes to mind is selling advertisements for a free TV guide. My sister and I were teammates on this venture. Our plan was to sell advertisements to local businesses. We contracted with a professional printing company to put the ads and TV guides together. We would contact the local grocery stores and other places with heavy traffic and put our free TV guides in their stores. Customers would pick them up. As they use the TV guides, they would see the ads and shop with the local merchants.

This is how we made money. This was during the early 1990s. We purchased one thousand TV guides for $1000. If we collected over $1,000 in ads, we made a profit. If we sold less than $1000 in ads, we lost money. We had about twenty pages worth of ad space. Our goal was to make $5000 per week in ads. We calculated we needed to earn $250 a page to equal $5000. That is $250, times 20 pages equals $5000. We sold full-page ads for $250, half page ads for $150, one-fourth page ads for $80, and one-eighth page ads for $45. Sounds a little complicated, but it worked. We published the TV guides weekly. We asked our advertisers to commit to at least three months. Most stayed longer. We collected the first month in advance. Subsequent months were to be collected about fifteen days before the upcoming month.

Here is how we sold the ads. We went to grocery stores and picked up other free publications. No one already had free TV guides. That was good. We studied the size, prices, and types of the ads, and the kind of businesses already advertising in the other papers. We thought it would be easier to sell to people that were already advertising. Each of us created a sales pitch to say on the phone. We called the businesses.

My typical phone call went something like this, "Hi, my name is Freda, and I'm selling ads for a free local TV guide. I will be in your area Monday afternoon and I would like to stop in and show the owner or manager a sample of our free TV guide and see if you would like to place an ad with us?" Then, I would pause and wait for a response.

Typical "no" responses would be:

- I am not interested.
- I have already spent my advertising budget for the year. Call me later.
- The owner or manager is not available.

Initially most of the responses were this kind. I thanked them for their time and moved on.

Typical "maybe" or "yes" responses would be:

- Can you come by around one?
- How much are the ads?
- Who else is advertising with you?
- How many people will the ads reach?
- What area do you cover?

For our first appointment, we did not even have an actual TV guide. We had a sample layout, a price list, and a belief that God would grant us success. We gathered information on our potential customer's business, cut out a sample of the ad he had placed in the other paper, dressed professionally, and showed up a few minutes early for our appointment. We were nervous but confident.

We made our first sale. After that, our confidence soared. The next day we made another sale. Then we went door to door in that shopping center. Most said no, but a few said come back later and another bought an advertisement. Before long, we sold enough to fill our whole book. We sent the ads to the printer and picked up our TV Guides a week later.

In the meantime, we spoke to the local grocery store managers. We thought it would be tough to get them to let us put our TV Guides in their stores. It was not. God had already gone before us and prepared the way. Most of them were pleased to be able to offer this to their customers for free. We only had to buy the stands and keep them full, which we did.

We met many small business owners. Most of them were gracious. They gave us referrals to their friends and commended us for our entrepreneurial spirit. A few tried to hire us as marketing reps for their businesses.

Our business ended about a year later when the printing company went out of business. The seasons were changing. The computer age was coming and the entire printing industry was about to be revamped. In addition, satellite TV was coming, and the TV guides would be on the TV screen. My sister and I were already pursuing other interests. We were discerning the times and making the necessary moves for the next stage of our lives. We visited all of our customers and thanked them for doing business with us. We visited with the grocery store managers, thanked them, and removed our stands.

LEARNING FROM MY DAD

When I was a child and our family business was slow, my dad would load up merchandise in his car and go up and down the streets selling. One day when I was with him, he was selling purses. He loaded many purses on his arms and we went into a crowded Laundromat. To my amazement, he sold them all in less than twenty minutes.

Sometimes, people are scared to be bold for fear of rejection. In my experience, this is hardly ever the reality. Most of the time people are friendly, if you are friendly to them. Most of the time, they will buy, if you offer them something they want. My dad was also a preacher and well respected in the community. He loved people and people loved him. If you respect yourself, people will respect you.

Sometimes people would come in our store with a sad story and ask for money. My dad would listen and offer them advice. Often that was exactly what they needed. Other times, he would take them to the side, reach into his pocket, and discreetly hand them some money. Most of all, they just needed to know that someone cared about them. That is what God does for us. Sometimes He gives us a word to guide us. Sometimes He gives us provision. Most of all, He lets us know that He cares about us.

My dad started several businesses in his lifetime. He became successful in many ways. He helped other people to start their own businesses, churches, and ministries. Since we all exist on this planet together and we all have hopes and dreams, then whenever possible, we must reach out and help one another. It makes us stronger and it makes life better.

My dad remarried when I was seven years old and I was happy to have a stepmother. I was born Milwaukee, Wisconsin and lived there until I was eight. Then, my family moved to Los Angeles. We moved to Dallas when I was seventeen. I live in the Dallas area today.

When I was a teenager, my family and I spent most of our summers traveling across the country as vendors at conventions. It was exciting and I looked forward to seeing the different cities. Most of the conventions we went to were church related. We had the chance to see many of the dynamic speakers and singers of the time. I learned how to book conventions and make travel arrangements, select and order products, and coordinate all the related activities. I learned how to talk and sell to people who were much older than I was. I learned to feel comfortable being the boss.

Conventioneers are usually on vacation and the atmosphere is relaxed and friendly. People come expecting to spend money, but they want a good value for their money. The best items to sell to travelers are things that are easy to transport in suitcases such as:

- Small personal items including jewelry and t-shirts
- new styles and trends that are not available yet in stores
- souvenirs of the city or state
- unique and artistic items created by the vendor
- original works such as CDs, DVDs, or books created by the vendor
- items related to the topic of the event such as religious items at a church convention, or home improvement gadgets at a home improvement convention

This is just an example of some ideas. It is not all-inclusive or exclusive. Some people will buy large items they see displayed, if they can have them delivered to their home.

If you have an original creation, you must be mindful of your pricing structure. Many inventors or creators of artistic items initially tend to overprice their items. They may be valuable to you or have cost a lot of make, but you cannot expect to recoup your whole investment at one time. It is advisable to have other items to sell, just in case your creation does not sell as well as you thought. Sometimes you are at the wrong event, or it is the wrong time.

HOME HEALTH CARE

I grew up and went to college. I earned a bachelor's degree in nursing. When I chose my major, I told my dad I did not want to be an entrepreneur anymore. I just wanted to do something to help people. Someone else would handle all the responsibilities of keeping the business going. I could just showed up do my work and go home.

My first year out of school I realized something was wrong. I loved my patients and the other nurses, but **I kept figuring out how to do things so much better**. Over the years, I kept going from one hospital to another looking for the one that was "doing things right." I got frustrated and probably frustrated many people around me.

I started a home health agency. My husband and I were partners. We started the office in our home. It cost $875 to get a license. Since I was already, a RN we did not have to hire one and that saved a lot of money. Within a few months, we outgrew the home and moved into an office building. Within three years, we had over fifty employees and well over a million dollars in revenue.

The company grew too fast. Before we had time to learn one lesson, there were many more that needed to be learned. It was a very serious business. The life and comfort of people were at stake. I did not take my responsibility lightly. It was also a heavily regulated business with a tremendous amount of paperwork. I built a loving and caring nursing staff that the patients loved, so more kept coming and coming. We went over and above for them. We bought beds for them when they could not afford them. We had leaky roofs fixed for patients who had no one to help them. We even paid for a funeral or two. We also went out of way for our employees to create an "ideal" working environment. They enjoyed their jobs and made a lot of money.

We made our money by sending health care providers into the home and billing Medicare for reimbursement at a pre-determined rate. That meant that we spent our money first and waited for reimbursement. Then, the United States Congress changed the reimbursement laws through the Health Care Reform Act, which essentially put most of the small agencies out of business. The reimbursement rate was slashed so low it would no longer cover the cost to pay the healthcare providers.

We protested. We went all the way to Capitol Hill with our trade association lobbyists, but we failed. **We tried to appeal to Congress based on compassion for the elderly. We had industry reports, expert testimonies, and heartfelt stories.** The Congressmen listened, but they were more interested in what was going on down the hall. The managed care lobbyists, our opposition at the time, were wining and dining them with expensive lobster dinners and champagne. We were out of our league. The seasons were changing. Manage care was coming to our industry and the small companies were squeezed out. We even filed a class action lawsuit in federal court, but we still lost. The judge said Congress had a right to enact any laws it wanted, and someone was always hurt.

We fought a good fight, but in the end, we did not prevail. It was time to move on to the next phase of our lives. We made a plan to close the business and transferred our patients and staff to other facilities. My family spent the next year healing. The lessons we learned were invaluable and we have made full use of them.

DEFINING SUCCESS

Different people define success in different ways. Each one of us must figure out what success is to us. **You will not know if you are successful, if you have not defined what it looks like to you**. Is it measured in money? Is a hundred thousand, a million, ten million dollars enough? How hard do you want to work for it? What are you willing to give up? What do you want to bring into your life that you do not already have? What do you want to remove from your life True success is a gift from God. We know it in our spirit before we can define it in words or works.

During my years of nursing, I met many elderly people who had reached the end of their lives. Some had made a lot of money and could afford the best healthcare, but they had no family or friends around them. Others never made much money. They had family and friends around, but they could not afford decent healthcare. They relied on the government to take care of them. In the end, they both described themselves as successful.

Today, I operate a successful Insurance agency with the help of my family. It is eight years old and peaceful. Most of our income is passive. I have learned that it is much better to build slowly with a good foundation. We have learned valuable lessons about balancing our business and our personal lives. We have built management systems into both. We work hard, but the work is enjoyable. We have great customers. From the beginning of our business, people have said God told them to come to us. We lay claim to our territory in the kingdom of God and continue to advance it at a steady pace.

Most of us will not build worldwide companies or ministries. We will not have household names, but we will be well known in our corner of the world. We will become pillars in our community. We will stand up as testimonies to what God is able to do in our lives. People will believe that if God can do it for us He can do it for them. They will have hope. We will be role models and community leaders to the generations coming after us. We will be beacons of light pointing the way. Directly and indirectly, we will affect the lives of so many people that we may never meet. We will do exactly what God has called us to do to advance His kingdom. We will be humble not arrogant. I define that as success.

Let us pray

God direct our path. Lead us to select a product or service that is honorable and desirable to you. Guide our path to those whom we can serve. Make our work productive. Give us a joyful heart that we may bring your light to those we touch. Lord, we honor you and worship you in all that we do. Money is the weapon you have given us to break the bondage of poverty and build generational wealth. Go before us and prepare our way. This we ask in your son Jesus' name, Amen.

Key Points to Remember

- The art of selling is learned

- Practice selling with a friendly crowd
- Provide good customer service
- Never put profits before people
- Set a fair price and write it down
- Present your product, answer questions, ask for the sale, and be quiet
- Explain your product in terms of how it provides value to the customer
- Time your orders to coincide with your event
- Keep an inventory log
- Keep money in a secure place
- Satisfied customers will do your best marketing
- Select simple products and services for your first business
- Pray and ask God to go before you
- Define what success means to you

Notes

4

Financial Planning

But seek ye first the kingdom of God,
and his righteousness;

and all these things shall be added unto you.

Matthew 6:33

FINANCIAL STATEMENTS

The three financial statements that business owners need to become familiar with are the income statement, the cash flow statement, and the balance sheet. These are periodic reports that summarize the financial affairs of the business. They are standardized reports required by lending institutions and investors. As the business grows, they become progressively more complicated and important. Computer programs make this task simpler.

We will use the figures from our sample business. We will assume that we sold our entire stock to simplify our financial records. However, in the real world, this hardly ever happens. Your may sell ninety percent of your stock, but when it gets too low it is hard to sell the rest. This can happen for a variety of reasons such as; you may not have the right size, style, or color. Include any leftover inventory on your financial records. First, we will complete the inventory log and add a column for the daily receipts. This information helps us complete the financial statements.

Starting Inventory		Number Sold	Balance	Amount Earned
T-shirts				
2XL	15	15	0	$150.00
1XL	20	20	0	$200.00
Large	10	10	0	$100.00
Small	15	10	0	$150.00
Sunglasses 50		50	0	$250.00
Toys 50		50	0	$150.00
Total				$1,000.00

Proverbs 24:3-4 says, *by wisdom a house is built, and through understanding it is established, through knowledge its rooms are filled.* We need to define of a few business terms to make sure we are talking the same language.

- Assets-anything owned that has value; resources of a person or business

- Dozen as a measurement—twelve
- Gross as a measurement—twelve dozen or 144
- Liability-the debt of a business
- Net worth or equity—resources of a business minus its debts
- Profits, earnings, and net income mean the same thing—what is left over after all the costs and expenses are subtracted
- Revenue, gross income, and sales mean the same thing—the amount of money brought into a company by its business activities.

An income statement shows the profitability of the company. It does not show a complete picture. It reports on what was sold and what it cost to sell it for a certain period, a month, a quarter, or a year. The basic formula is Sales—Costs & Expenses = Net Income.

Simplified Income Statement sample

Start up loan from owner	$ 500.00
Sales Revenue	$ 1,000.00
Total income	$ 1,500.00
Cost of goods sold	$ 400.00
Booth rent	$ 100.00
Start up loan repayment	$ 500.00
Total expenses	$ 1,000.00
Net income (profit)	$ 500.00

A cash flow statement tracks how money moves through the company for a certain period. It is probably the most familiar financial statement, because it is like balancing a checkbook.

Simplified cash flow statement sample (like balancing a checkbook)

Date	Description	deposit	withdrawal	balance
	Owners contribution	$500.00		$500.00

Booth rent		$100.00	$400.00
Payment to suppliers:			
T-shirts		$240.00	$160.00
Sunglasses		$100.00	$60.00
Toys		$50.00	$10.00
Shipping		$10.00	-
Revenue from sales	$1,000.00		$1,000.00

The balance sheet shows the worth of the company. What it has, minus what it owes, equals what it is worth. That is the net worth or equity. The balance sheet must always balance. If you add an asset, you must also add a liability or increase the equity. The balance sheet reports the worth of the company for a particular period, usually for the day it was done. Unsold inventory is included as an asset on the balance sheet because it is owned by the business. Unpaid invoices are listed as liabilities.

Simplified Balance Sheet sample:

Formula: Assets—liabilities= equity
Assets=
Cash in bank $1000.00
Inventory
$0
Liabilities=
Start up loan $500.00

$1000—$500= $500 equity
Assets—liabilities= equity (net worth)

EXIT/GROWTH STRATEGY OPTIONS

After we have sold our inventory, we will come to a point where we must evaluate our lives and where we want to go with our business. You must communicate with God. You have to determine if this is the right season of your life to move forward in this direction or if God is speaking to you about something else. You should include your options in your business plan and include what factors will influence your decisions later. You should state those factors as clearly as possible.

First option, you can decide to cash out and close this business. You pay back the loan with interest, divide the profits among the owners, and go your separate ways. If there were three owners, financial statements would look like this:

Cash flow statement (like balancing a checkbook)

Description	deposit	withdrawal	balance
Owners Contribution	500.00		$500.00
Payment To supplier		($400.00)	$100.00
Booth Rent		($100.00)	.00
Revenue From sales	$1000.00		$1000.00
Loan repayment		($500.00)	$500.00
10% Interest On loan		($50.00)	$450.00
Owner # 1 Earnings		($150.00)	$300.00
Owner # 2 Earnings		($150.00)	$150.00
Owner # 3 Earnings		($150.00)	$.00

One variation of this is that one owner buys out the other owners and continues the business. He pays interest on the loan, but not the entire loan. The owner(s) who made the loan is entitled to a return on investment (ROI). A written agreement is needed with payback terms of the loan. This profit and loss statement (also called income statement) would look like this:

Income statement:

Start up loan	$500.00
Sales revenue	$1000.00
Total income	$1500.00
Cost of goods sold	$400.00
Booth rent	$100.00
10% interest on loan	$50.00
Owner # 1 earnings	$150.00
Owner # 2 earnings	$150.00
Total expenses	$850.00
Net Income	$650.00

The second option is to continue the business just as it is. The owners may make changes to the product line or the marketing strategy here and there, but it is essentially run the same. In our example, we spent $500 made $1000 and profited $500. Depending on how hard you want to work, you can continue this process as often as desired. It could also be run as a home based business or Internet business.

If you want to travel, you can become a vendor and travel to trade shows and conventions all over the country. Most major cities have them going on weekly, if not daily. The Internet, convention centers, hotels, and trade magazines are good ways to find what convention is where. Usually, the best source is other vendors. They can tell you which conventions are profitable and which are not. Many people operate businesses like this for years. There is nothing wrong with this. I once made $1000 in one day selling $2.00 hair bows at a national convention. It is time to release your creativity, see what is not there, and call it into being. Have fun and enjoy the cities as you travel. Whenever possible help the less fortunate.

PLANNING YOUR FINANCES

The third option is to expand your entrepreneurial pursuits. This will take the greatest effort and offers the greatest rewards. In an ongoing business, the initial $500 borrowed for start-up (usually from the owner(s)) goes back into the business along with some of the profit to buy more inventories, and pay overhead expenses. We evaluate the products and make any necessary changes. We will talk more about that throughout the remainder of the book.

You will need the services of an accountant early on. You may not need him or her to keep your records, but you at least need their services to advise you on taxes. In our sample business, we left off taxes to simplify our example. In the real world, you cannot do this. The government requires sales tax collected on products sold. There are specific requirements on how to deposit the taxes and file tax forms. Contact your state office and the IRS for specific instructions. My advice is to learn as much as you can for yourself. It is better to grow your business slowly, so you will have time to learn. **Never, ever, ever turn your books over to anyone and not know what is going on with them**. You must always have access to your financial records and know what the numbers mean, and how they affect you.

Spot-check the statements against your actual receipts or records. **You must establish a good checks and balance system to keep people honest**, even partners and advisors. This is a major problem when dealing with cash and requires much wisdom. If you do not know how to read the financial reports correctly, or comply with the tax laws you must learn. As your business grows, the financial reports and taxes will become more and more complex.

You may be so busy running your business that you turn over to someone else the responsibility of keeping up your financial records and filing your taxes. You must still increase your financially literacy. You can take a course online or at a community college. You can buy a book and read it, and read it and read it again until you understand it. If you still cannot understand it, buy an easier book. **If you have to go all the way down to, financial literacy for first graders then start there**. The point is that wherever you are do not stay there. Set your heights higher and keep on climbing. Eventually, you will notice that God is right there with you helping you.

BUDGETING

Researchers say that sixty percent the people who write out a budget will abandon it by the second month. Many more never even bother to write one. The reasons that people give for not sticking to them is that they are too complicated, annoying, and restrictive. However, a well thought out financial strategy can help you achieve your goals. It has been my experience that most people do not have a problem with the basic budget formula. You make a list of your expected income, write your expected expenses, and see what is left. Most people get in trouble when they do not plan for an unexpected change in the expected income or their expected expenses and the numbers no longer balance.

Entrepreneurs know this all too well, especially during the start up phase. That is why it is imperative to keep your overhead expenses as low as possible for as long as possible. You should be in no hurry to go out and create bills just to look good and impress other people. Every dollar you plant back into your business is a seed that has the potential to produce a hundred or even a thousand fold return.

You have to plan for the unexpected. In the example we used as a vendor, a number things could go wrong. Some you can control and some you cannot.

Some things you cannot control are:

- The expected crowd just does not show up for one reason or another.
- The weather changes from hot and sunny to cold and rainy and rainy.

- Every single vendor shows up selling the exact same products that you are selling.
- A national emergency causes the cancellation of the entire event.

Even if some these unexpected events happen, you do not lose your investment or your inventory. You just move on to the next event. God will guide you, if you ask Him.

Unexpected events do not just happen to entrepreneurs. Just the other day, a friend shared his story. He went to work on Friday morning, which was payday, and found the whole company locked with chains around the doors. The police were in front preventing anyone from entering. The company went out of business with no warning to the several hundred employees. They were out in the cold with no paychecks and no jobs. There had been no indication that the company was even in financial trouble!

The point is that you have to put together a written financial plan that works for you. You have to put some cushion in that plan. You cannot spend down to your last dollar, or even your last one hundred dollars, and one day not even your last thousand dollars.

If you have an old car, keep it in good shape. It may be a while before you will buy a new one. The same goes for your home keep it neat and clean and in good shape. You may need to stay there a while longer. Of course, if you can get out from under any debt, you should do it. **The best investment you can make right now is in your own business.** One day your business will be successful and the money will flow like milk and honey. That will be the time to buy a nice car and a nice house. You will be spending out of your overflow. In the beginning, your money is your seed. The more seeds you plant the greater the harvest.

Financial Growth

In our example as a vendor, we spent $500 and made $500 more. That is a one hundred percent increase. You could take that same $500 and keep sowing it back into your business. After ten times, that same $500 will have made $5,000. That is a one thousand percent increase, and you still have the original $500. No one is going to pay you that kind of increase on an investment of $500. You have to be smart and see the wisdom in building your own business. If you can look down the road and see the brighter days ahead, then you will have the courage and resolve to deal with the problems of today.

It is very important to build a business that you enjoy and has the potential to be very profitable. Since initially, most of the profits will need to go back into the business to earn greater profits. Our first goal was to spend $500 and earn $1000 with at a $500 profit. We can move on from here. For instance:

- Goal #2 spend $1000 earn $2000 and profit $1000
- Goal #3 spend $1500 earn $3000 and profit $1500
- Goal #4 spend $2000 earn $4000 and profit $2000
- Goal #5 spend $2500 earn $5000 and profit $2500
- Goal #6 spend $3000 earn $6000 and profit $3000

If you increase your goals slowly and methodically, you will see what is working and what is not without risking too much. In order to reinvest your profits back into your business, you are going to have to do whatever you are doing now to support yourself a little while longer. In this example, the goals and profits fit into neat rows, but in reality, they hardly ever work out this way. You may make it to goal number three and have to stay there for a while before you make it to number four. You will probably have some setbacks and wind up back at two and struggle to get back to four. You do not have to push faster than you want to go. The goals can be measured in months or years. It is your business, you decide.

Setting goals and achieving them is easier, if you are building a business that you enjoy. **Your passion will drive you**. However, you still have to be objective and evaluate if your products are appealing to a broad enough customer base to be profitable. You will also have to keep developing marketplaces. The example, of a vendor at the community festival, was a good place to start, but at some point, you will grow beyond community events.

You will over saturate your marketplace and your growth will be marginal. If you decide to continue as a vendor, you will need to start going to state or national conventions. The attendance may be around 50,000 people instead of 5,000. You will need more money for inventory and booth rent. You will need to write out a plan for meeting that goal including making sure your inventory matches the event. Some of the vendor spaces at the large conventions may sell out a year or two in advance.

Open a business checking account to deposit money and pay business expenses. If possible, separate the money you are saving into a money market account, so it earns interest as you continue to build. You do not need to lock your money into an account that penalizes you to make a withdrawal. Again, you will get a much greater return by investing in your business than any investment account at this time. The time will come when you will need to learn how to invest your money wisely and earn passive income.

The same money principles apply to service or information oriented businesses. Your profits may even increase faster, because you do not have to invest in inventory. You have to be mindful of your pricing structure. If your price is too low, you will have too much work and not enough profit to hire help. If your price is too high, your competition will move in, undercut your prices, and steal your customers.

Key Points to remember

- The three standardized financial statements typically required by lenders and investors are the income statement, cash flow statement and a balance sheet
- Increase your financial literacy in order to grow
- Learn more about taxes
- Open a business checking account and separate personal and business funds
- The best investment you can make at this time is in your own business

- Set goals for growth according to your definition of success
- Continuously monitor your prices to stay competitive

Notes

5

Money Management

But seek ye first the kingdom of God,
and his righteousness;

and all these things shall be added unto you.

Matthew 6:33

MONEY MANAGEMENT

In Luke 19: 12-27, Jesus said:

> *A certain nobleman went into a far country to receive for himself a kingdom, and to return.*
>
> *And he called his ten servants, and delivered them a pound, and said unto them, Occupy till I come.*
>
> *But his citizens hated him, and sent a message after him, saying, We will not have this man to reign over us.*
>
> *And it came to pass, that when he returned, having received his kingdom, then he commanded these servants to be called unto him, to whom he had given the money, that he might know how much every man had gained by trading.*
>
> *Then came the first, saying, Lord thy pound has gained ten pounds.*
>
> *And he said unto him Well, thou good servant: Because thou has been faithful in a very little have thou authority over ten cities.*
>
> *And the second came, saying, Lord, thy pound hath gained five pounds.*
>
> *And he said likewise to him, Be thou also over five cities.*
>
> *And another came, saying, Lord, Behold, here is thy pound, which I have kept laid up in a napkin:*
>
> *For I feared thee, because thou art an austere man: thou takest up that thou layedst not down, and reapest that thou didst not sow.*
>
> *And he said unto him, Out of thine own mouth will I judge thee, thou wicked servant. Thou knewest that I was an austere man, taking up that I laid not down, and reaping that I did not sow:*
>
> *Wherefore then gavest not thou my money into the bank, that at my coming I might have required mine own with usury?*
>
> *And he said unto them that stood by, Take from him the pound, and give it to him that hath ten pounds.*

And they said unto him, Lord, he hath ten pounds.

For I say unto you, That ***unto every one which hath shall be given,*** *and from him that hath not, even that he hath shall be taken away from him.*

But those mine enemies, which would not that I should reign over them, bring hither, and slay them before me."

In Mark 2:21-22 Jesus says,

No man also seweth a piece of new cloth on an old garment: else, the new piece that filled it up taketh away from the old, and the rent is made worse.

And ***no man putteth new wine into old bottles: else the new wine doth burst the bottles,*** *and the wine is spilled, and the bottles will be marred: but new wine must be put into new bottles.*

There are many important lessons here. Notice that the first servant said your pound has gained ten pounds. Then, the second said your pound has gained five pounds. A pound is gaining pounds or **a little bit of money is gaining more money. Money will multiply**. The nobleman's instruction to the servants was to occupy until he comes, which means to do business. We know this because when the nobleman returned as king he wanted to know how much each man had gained by trading.

This is a lesson about how to grow a business. If you put into practice the principles we have already talked about in the previous chapters, God has already given you what you need to start. To some he has given the ability to gain ten pounds from one, some the ability to gain five pounds from one, and some he has given one pound and expects to at least gain interest on that pound. It does not matter how much He gives you to start with. He is concerned with how effectively you use it to gain more. He said the third servant was wicked because he did not operate in faith. Instead, he allowed fear to paralyze him to the point that he did nothing. He had no more to lose than the others did, and still he did not even try.

This concept is the new wine. You need wine bottles in order to receive it. Money cannot multiply if not put to work. If you simply take your money and spend it on things that will not produce more money, how can it work for you? This is so important to God that He takes away the one pound from the third servant and gives it to the first. **It appears that in the kingdom of God, the rich do get richer.**

Let us look at another example. Let us say you earn $2000 per month after taxes. By the time, you pay your rent or mortgage, your electricity, phone, car payment, and insurance you have $400 left. By the time, you buy food and gas and a few other things there is nothing left. Your money has been taken away from you. It is working for the property owner or Mortgage Company, the electric company, Phone Company, car finance company, insurance company, grocery store owner, and the Gasoline Company. They have learned to put money to work. You have learned to go to work and pay them.

Now, most people will say, I have to have a place to live, a car to drive, insurance, gas, lights, phone, and food. That is correct you do, and you could spend the rest of your life working for those things. If you choose to do so, that is fine.

You can also choose to do some things differently. You can pull five hundred dollars out of your paycheck at a strategic time, plant it as a seed into your business, make another five hundred dollars off that five hundred and use that extra five hundred dollars to pay your bills. That gives you an additional five hundred you did not have before, and your bills are still paid. Then, you keep reinvesting those five hundred dollars to earn more profits.

If this sounds too risky, you can start with one hundred dollars. The amount does not matter. It is more important that you understand the concept of how to make money work for you. It is impossible to have success at any level without sacrifice. God is not trying to take anything from you. He is trying to give to you, but He can only give to you according to your level of faith. Your faith increases as your knowledge and experiences with Him increase.

Building a business is not a get rich quick scheme. It is about building through a well thought out systematic plan. You have to honestly evaluate yourself and your lifestyle and determine what needs to change to take you where want to go. If you increase your expenses at the same rate as your income, where are you going? Let us look at this example:

Income	expenses	excess
$1000	$800	$200 or 20%
$2000	$1600	$400 or 20%
$10,000	$8,000	$2,000 or 20%
$100,000	$80,000	$20,000 or 20%

One day I saw a news program where a NFL football player was protesting his salary of $3,000,000 per year. He said he needed more money, because he had *kids to feed*. They showed his home. It was a $10,000,000 mansion. He lived alone. The two kids lived with their mother!

This situation reaches down to the core of an individual. Many people say they want financial freedom, but their actions are far from it. They buy things they cannot afford and are in the bondage of debt. Once they pay off something, they quickly replace that payment with other payments and the cycle continues. It seems most people are more comfortable with excessive debt than financial freedom.

This is only part of the problem. There are powerful spiritual, physical, and mental forces at work to keep this system of debt in place. If you do not plan your life, someone else will plan it for you. You will be part of someone else's plan for their benefit. If this is the case with you right now, do not get angry, get a revelation. God is trying to tell you something. It is doubtful that you will be successful at growing your business, if you do not spend your money wisely. There are whole industries devoted to helping people understand how to budget, manage debt, buy wiser, and save. **There is nothing wrong with managed debt if it you use it strategically**

to make more money. Education trumps ignorance. Devote yourself to learning. If you fight, God will help you.

PARTNERING WITH GOD

Many people work on jobs for which they have no passion. They say they work in order to "pay their bills." What would happen if they had no bills or even half their current bills? Is it possible they would re-create (recreate) their jobs? Would there be a need to buy so many "things" they could not afford? Would our economy fail or thrive? What kingdom are we building?

These are not new questions. They are as old as humanity, maybe older. Satan led a revolution in heaven. The bible tells us that one third of the angels in heaven chose to follow Satan. You must choose which kingdom you really want. Jesus said we cannot put a new patch on an old garment; eventually the new patch will shrink down, pull at the tear, and make it worse. Some bad habits cannot be patched. They have to be completely removed. Ultimately, you must make this a personal matter. Jesus will judge the intent of the heart. He is able to remove anything you sincerely ask Him to remove. He said, a tree is known by the fruit it bears. Cherry trees produce cherries. Apple trees produce apples. The children of God should produce fruit that advances the kingdom of God.

Consider the example of a magnet and paper clips. The paper clips lay dormant until a magnet moves over them. The magnet draws the paper clips to it by simply passing by them. The magnet always had the ability to draw. The paper clips were always attracted. Nothing happened until the magnet moved into position.

Meditate on this then ask yourself, how do I move into position? The answer is in the Word of God, and it is simpler than you think. Let us look at one more scripture.

Habakkuk 2:1-3 KJV says:

> *I will stand upon my watch, and set me upon the tower, and will watch to see what He will say unto me, and what I shall answer when I am reproved.*
>
> *And the Lord answered me, and said, write the vision, and make it plain upon tablets, that he may run that readeth it.*
>
> *For the vision is yet for an appointed time, but at the end it shall speak, and not lie: though it tarry, wait for it; because it will surely come, it will not tarry.*

Let us take a closer look:

I will stand upon my watch—like a soldier, actively looking for something, disciplined, not sitting down, not sleeping, and not wandering off.

And set me upon the tower—above what I can see at eye level, looking into the distance, not my present surrounding.

And will watch to see what He says to me—Expect God to answer at any moment. Believe that He has the answer for whatever you need.

And what I shall say when I am reproved—I have missed opportunities before and blamed everybody else, even God, can I now learn and move on?

And the Lord answered me—He will answer. He is answering right now.

*And said, **write the vision***—you will receive a vision from God. Follow his instruction and write it down.

And make it plain upon tablets—the vision becomes clearer and focused when written down, keep a writing tablet nearby

That he may run who readeth it—the vision comes to you but it will affect many others—it is important to your success that you clearly direct them.

For the vision is yet for an appointed time—the vision will lead you into your future

But at the end it shall speak and not lie—it will happen just like God said it would

Though it tarry wait for it—patience builds character, keep learning while you are waiting

For it will surely come and not tarry—It will be right on time when it comes. Joseph's vision took over twenty years to come to fruition

You must spend time reading the word of God to understand how He talks to His children. **As you grow in the Lord, your discernment will grow**. As opportunities arise, and they will, you will be able to instantly speak to the Lord and know whether you are hearing His voice guiding you. It takes studying and praying to walk by faith. We may start out with a blind faith. As we mature, our faith grows from our solid knowledge and experience with God. You will return to this scripture many times. Other visions will come. Our God is a living God. He is constantly leading and guiding us.

If you can submit to God's will, you will hear from Him. He will speak to you personally making you a magnet that attracts the things you want into your life. He will put people and resources around you to help. If you actively seek, you will find. If you knock and keep on knocking, the doors will open.

The business to which God has called you to is one that He has already gifted you to be able to build. In other words, He is probably not calling you to start an accounting firm if you are not good with numbers. However if you are good with numbers and lack the necessary education to be an accountant, He may be directing you back to school to get the credentials to become an accountant. Then, you can start your own firm. Whatever it is, trust that the Holy Spirit will guide you, and He is able to open the doors. Above all, believe in your heart that God is love and wants only the very best for you.

Jeremiah 29:11says,

> *for I know the thoughts I think toward you, saith the Lord, thoughts of peace, and not of evil, to give you an expected end.*
>
> *Then shall ye call upon me, and ye shall go and pray unto me, and I will harken unto you.*

We must rely on the power of God to put His super on top of our natural abilities for supernatural results. **God desires his children to prosper financially**. He gives us peace as we prosper. He wants us to call upon Him and pray, and He wants to have a close personal relationship with us.

Financial Freedom

When your finances are not free, you are in a financial bondage, which affects your mental, physical, and spiritual condition. Firstly, mental bondage saying things like, I cannot afford this or that so I frequently go without. You learn to live in a state of unworthiness instead of an abundant life as a child of God. Secondly emotional bondage, you feel like you are not as good as people who live in better neighborhoods and drive nicer cars and have nicer "things." How can you effectively witness to them? God is calling you to be bold. He said to go into all the world and preach the gospel. Thirdly, physical bondage, you are unable to buy what you need to take care of your physical body. You are also restricted physically to certain neighborhoods and unable to travel where and when you want to for leisure or ministry needs. **Jesus came to set the captives free. He came, died, and rose again to set us free from all types of bondage**. He loves us, and He wants us to live abundant and free lives. This includes having the money we need to accomplish all that He will put in us to accomplish for His glory.

He does not leave us alone to fend for ourselves. He provides. If you look back over your life, can you honestly say that God failed you? Most of the messes we got into we caused by our own bad decisions usually based on excessive fear, excessive greed, excessive lust, or excessive pride. We jumped straight in, and then demanded that God get us out. God never said he would be our personal genie and grant our every wish. Sometimes godly people are genuinely confused and hurt. Sometimes the people inside the church building are too quick to condemn instead of comfort and teach. But if you continue to cry out to God, you will see that even in the hard times He is there and leading you to the next level of your life. God is love and He loves you. He has compassion and restoration for the wearied soul. Once restored, He expects you to turn around and help the ones coming after you. Freely you have received so freely you are to give.

RECOVERY FROM FAILURE

You *can* recover from failure. The first thing you have to do is recognize that you have failed. This may sound like an obvious thing, but **one of the hardest things for godly people to do is to recognize that they have failed.** The next deal will not set it all straight. It is over, finished, the curtain has gone down and failure is all around. The money that you were expecting did not come. The opportunity has passed.

Before you sink into a deep state of depression, you have to remember that there is a God and He is still on the throne. You have to talk to Him. You have to cry out to Him. It is in some of the darkest moments of failure that you are truly able to hear from God. God did not cause you to fail. You are responsible. You have to accept that. If not, you will go on for years and years blaming everybody and everything else including God. **As soon as you accept responsibility, you are on your way to wholeness.**

How do you accept responsibility? You have to evaluate what happened. You must take an honest look at all the pieces. You should write down as much as you can. It helps you sort out things. You can only store a limited amount of information in your head. When your business has failed, there seems to be an unending list of people to tell you why it failed. In the end, the only voice that matters is yours. Do you understand where you went wrong or even that you went wrong?

You may not be the only one responsible, but you will not be able to move on until you can accept your part. **You can ask God to help see what your part is and is not**. You are not alone. That helps if you tend to be extra hard on yourself. Most of the great people in the bible failed at one thing or another. Many of them failed repeatedly. Paul, who wrote many of the books of the New Testament, failed at being the righteous man he thought he was. He thought he was doing the will of God, persecuting Christians, until he met Jesus on the road to Damascus. Moses, who God used to give us the Ten Commandments and the rest of the law, failed as a leader of the Israelites. He led them in circles in the desert for forty years, and God never allowed him to enter into the promise land. David, the man after God's own heart, failed at controlling the desires of his flesh. He committed adultery and then had Bathsheba's husband killed. Peter, who walked on water and walked and talked with Jesus daily, swore he would never disown him, but he did on three occasions on the morning of Jesus' crucifixion.

Most successful entrepreneurs have had at least one business failure before they became successful. **Failure is not bad, and it may even be a precursor to success.** It allows us to understand that we are not all knowing. It helps us to understand that we need to trust in God. Nobody wants to fail. Nobody says to himself that he will purposely set out to fail so he can trust God more. That would be insane. We intend to succeed. We intend to soar.

God's ways are not our ways and God is not a fool. You must recognize that you lack something and if you will allow Him, **God will build into you what is missing**. Even if your business failed simply because the whole industry failed, there was still something lacking in you that made you fail to see the seasons changing and plan your next move. Every one of those people of the bible God used in a great way before and after their failure. The only real failure is the failure to recognize the sovereignty of God. Once you come to terms with that, you can get back up and move on to higher heights. Many of the most valuable lessons in life we learn in the hard times.

Once you have gone through the grieving, evaluated what you did right and what you did wrong, **God can use you again**. It is time to stand on your feet, hold your head up high, and get back to work. Most entrepreneurs will start another business within a year or two. All the information you have learned is valuable and will be useful in your next venture. If you built too fast, you will learn to build slower. If you made too many decisions without enough knowledge, you will learn to be more diligent. It you trusted people you should not have, you will learn to be wiser. If you took off running and left God behind, you will learn to wait on Him. *For the vision is yet for an appointed time, but at the end it shall speak, and not lie: though it tarry, wait for it, because it will surely come, it will not tarry,* Habakkuk 2:3.

GOOD STEWARDSHIP

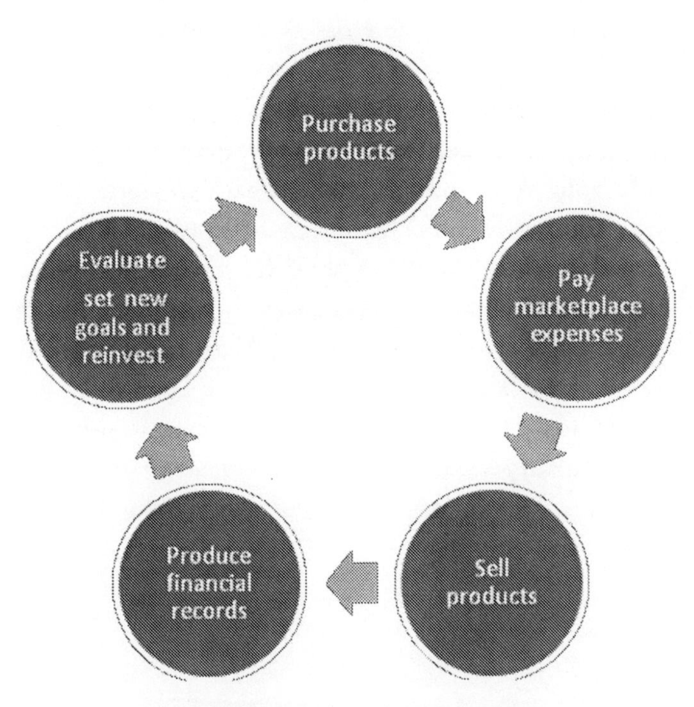

The business cycle of a wholesale/retailer.

The start-up phase of a business is so difficult, because you must learn to do so many new things. Sometimes they seem to happen all at the same time. In the example of the vendor, we did the phases one at a time. In reality there can be many things going on at the same time. You may have to plan for several consecutive events. Monday and Tuesday you are at one event, Thursday and Friday another and Saturday another. You have to put your organization skills in high gear. The customers at the events could be completely different. You have to make sure you have the right kind of products to appeal to the right customers. T-shirts, sunglasses, and water toys may appeal to the Saturday family oriented crowd. The Monday and Tuesday crowd may be a teachers' convention. While the Thursday and Friday crowd may be a church convention.

This could put a strain on your finances as you place orders for all three events at the same time. If you grow too fast and take on too much debt, you can run out of money. Unsold inventory is debt. It is money spent that is not collected on yet. You will have a cash flow problem if you are not careful, which is one of the major reasons that small businesses fail. The money goes out faster than it comes in. Sometimes entrepreneurs feel pressured to keep pushing forward because they have too many business or personal expenses.

This is a management problem, and you are the manager. You can try to borrow money and keep going, but think before you take on more debt. You must slow down long enough to evaluate your life. Are you on track with your goals or are you spinning out of control. Is God still guiding you? Have you left Him somewhere? It is in the very nature of the entrepreneur to want to grow and grow and grow. The wisdom and peace of God has to tame that nature or failure is just a short distance away. Many entrepreneurs do not fail because they cannot get their business up and running. Frequently, the opposite is true. Many fail because they are too successful and cannot manage their cash flow and all the other things that come with success.

Entrepreneurs and managers usually have different mindsets. The entrepreneur's gift is to build. He or she starts with very little and grows that into something great. The manager's gift is to take something already built and bring order and structure to it to make it stronger. Managers often buy businesses that entrepreneurs build. Managers create policies and procedures, hire and train staff, and chart a course to bring the company to maturity. Intrapreneur is a relatively new term but not a new concept. The intrapreneur's gift is to take on entrepreneur-like ventures within a large corporate body and expand into new territories.

Entrepreneurs have to develop some management skills or the company will not last long enough to sell to a manager. The entrepreneur will find himself in a constant state of building but never having much to show for it. That is why entrepreneurs must build slow and with a good foundation. We must trust in God. We must learn how to manage a growing business, money, and success. We must become good stewards.

A major part of money management is spending it in better ways. America is a nation of consumers. The irony is that **many business owners have made a great deal of money off other peoples' dysfunction**. We must avoid this. Once we know better, we can teach people how to make better decisions with their money. We must hold up a higher standard. We cannot be effective witnesses for Christ without integrity. Jesus said, what does it profit a man to gain the whole world and lose his own soul.

In Luke 11:24-26 Jesus said,

When the unclean spirit is gone out of man, he walketh through dry places, seeking rest; and finding none, he saith, I will return unto my house from whence I came out.

And when he cometh, he findeth it swept and garnished.

Then goeth he, and taketh to him seven other spirits more wicked that himself: and they enter in, and dwell there: and the last state of the man is worse than the first.

The problem you had with no money will magnify with money, and more problems will come and join them. As soon as you start to prosper, hell releases its hounds. Attacks come from all fronts. When the people of Judah faced opposition while trying to rebuild their city this is what they did:

Nehemiah 4:16-18

Half of the men worked, while the other half were equipped with spears, bows, and armor.

The officers posted themselves behind all the people of Judah who were building the wall.

Those who carried materials did their work with one hand and held a weapon in the other, and each of the builders wore his sword at his side as he worked.

Therefore:

- Build your business according to the plan God has given you.
- Build your life according to the revelatory word of God.
- Stay in fellowship with likeminded believers.
- Stand your ground and defend your territory.

Be on the lookout for the opposition. Sometimes it is obvious such as your competitors. Sometimes it is subtle such as jealous friends who passively undermine you.

Tithing and Committing to God

Tithing is the vehicle God gives us to advance to the next level. It is giving 10% back to the God that gave us the power to get the 100%. It is an act of worship. It says I care more about the God than the things. It moves our focus from the material world to the spiritual world. **It helps us to make wiser choices understanding that we are managers of God's money.**

It is indeed an honor and privilege to have the God of all creation care about us. We can believe that God will take us to higher heights, if we are faithful to Him. We owe Him everything, but He asks so little in return. Who would not love a God who loves us so much? Who would not want to live in His kingdom forever?

Have you ever paid for concert tickets online then went to the will call booth, picked up your tickets and went into the concert. This is what Jesus did. He paid the price. By faith, we believe that He did, claim our tickets and enter through the gate into the glorious kingdom of God. Once we see how great it is, we go and tell everyone who will listen about what we have found. We cannot keep silent. It is so wonderful. We see the whole world in a different way. Our lives transform. Our strength is renewed. We look for ways to help build the kingdom of God. Our small business begins to grow and we must move on in the power of God.

If you have read this far in this book without committing or recommitting your life to Christ, it has no doubt been very stressful. Jesus is willing. If you stretch out your hand to Him, He will guide you in safely. If He is tugging at your heart, do not let this opportunity slip away.

Romans 10:9-10 says that:

> *if you confess with your mouth Jesus as Lord, and believe in your heart that God raised Him from the dead, you will be saved.*
>
> *For with the heart a person believes and with the mouth confesses, resulting in salvation.*
>
> Joel 2:32 says,
>
> *Everyone who calls on the name of the Lord will be saved.*

Get alone with God. Ask him into your heart. Cry out to him. Confess your sins and lay them at his feet. The struggle is over. Jesus has already won the victory. Confront the problem. Claim the promises of God.

Key Points to Remember

- Money will make more money if put to work
- If you do not put your money to work for you, it will be taken away from you
- If you do not manage your money, someone else will manage it for you to their benefit
- God can make you a magnet to attract the things you want into your life
- Jesus came, died, and rose again to set us free from all kinds of bondage including financial bondage

- You can recover from failure
- You must develop management skills to bring stability to your business and hold your territory
- Tithing is an act of worship to God

Questions

- Think back over your life, do you have a problem with earning money or managing it?
- List some of your past mistakes with money.
- Has God revealed a vision to you about a business opportunity? Write it down.
- What are your next steps?
- As you begin to prosper, what opposition are you likely to face from the people close to you?
- Write down some countermeasures.
- Have you committed or recommitted your life to Christ?
- Are you tithing?
- How have you been faithful to God?
- List five private things that you are truly grateful to God for.
- Why do you want to start a business?

Notes

6

Moving On

But seek ye first the kingdom of God,
and his righteousness;

and all these things shall be added unto you.

Matthew 6:33

STRUCTURING A BUSINESS FOR GROWTH

This course is for people who have no chance of getting a bank loan, no collateral, and no money. If that was you, it will not always be you. As God raises you up as builders in His kingdom, you will go far beyond here.

In Matthew 6:14-16 ASV Jesus said,

> *Ye are the light of the world. A city that is set on an hill cannot be hid.*
>
> *Neither do men light a candle, and put it under a bushel, but on a candlestick; and it giveth light unto all that are in the house.*
>
> *Let your light so shine before men, that they may see your good works, and glorify your Father, which is in heaven.*

God will call you out of obscurity and into a public place to let your light shine. He *will* call you. If you are able to hear and answer, it is because God has chosen you.

In Matthew 22:1-14, **Jesus said it this way:**

> *The kingdom of heaven is like a certain king who arranged a marriage for his son,*
>
> *and sent out his servants to call those who were invited to the wedding; and they were not willing to come.*
>
> *Again, he sent out other servants, saying, Tell those who are invited, See, I have prepared my dinner; my oxen and fatted cattle are killed, and all things are ready. Come to the wedding.*
>
> *But they made light of it and went their ways, one to his own farm, another to his business.*
>
> *And the rest seized his servants, treated them spitefully, and killed them.*
>
> *But when the king heard about it, he was furious. And he sent out his armies, destroyed those murderers, and burned up their city.*

Then he said to his servants, 'The wedding is ready, but those who were invited were not worthy.

Therefore go into the highways, and as many as you find, invite to the wedding.

So those servants went out into the highways and gathered together all whom they found, both bad and good. And the wedding hall was filled with guests.

But when the king came in to see the guests, he saw a man there who did not have on a wedding garment.

So he said to him, Friend, how did you come in here without a wedding garment? And he was speechless.

Then the king said to the servants, Bind him hand and foot, take him away, and cast him into outer darkness; there will be weeping and gnashing of teeth.

For many are called, but few are chosen.

If you have a desire to claim territory in the kingdom of God though entrepreneurship, but you think you do not have enough money, experience, or education then read this story again. Sometimes the people who seem to be the most likely to succeed are too busy to do God's will. He will often choose ordinary people with willing and obedient hearts. He knew all about you when He called you. He knows what your limitations are and wants to show you what He can do with your life in spite of them. The scripture said he invited the good and the bad. He has called the good and the bad in you. You will grow in grace.

Continue to pray and write your prayers down, you will see that God is answering them. He is guiding you into His perfect will for your life. He has already placed everything in you that you need. He is now showing you how to get it out and become a kingdom builder. You have to study to develop sound business skills, but some lessons you can only learn by experience. The Holy Spirit can only reveal others. What is God revealing to you? Why did the king ask the man without the wedding clothes how he got in?

DEALING WITH PARTNERS

Many small businesses are started or expanded by partnerships. Choosing one, even if it is a spouse, is no easy task. I have known potential businesses that dissolved before they ever started, because the partners could not decide on a name for the business. I thought that was absurd. Then a year later, two others friends decided not to go into business, because they could not agree on whose name would be first. Certainly, each partner should bring something to the table that the other does not have. However, you cannot be total opposites. You have to agree on the fundamental things. You should have common goals and dreams, similar methods for getting there, similar belief systems, and similar definitions of success.

At the beginning stage of starting a business, your business partner should be someone you know fairly well. Later as your business grows, you can collaborate with people or entities that are distant. **You need to know your partner's strengths and weaknesses. You also need to know your own.** Are you an honest person? Is your partner? Are you good at managing money, or do you spend every dime that touches your hands. Are you a control freak? Is your partner? Do you or your partner have a tendency to be lazy? Do you or your partner have a problem with keeping commitments? Do you have integrity? Does your partner have integrity? Do you or your partner have hidden addictions that the stress of starting a business could trigger? What about later as the business makes money? If either of you are married, to other people, do you get along with the other's spouse. Even if you are both the same sex, the other spouses could still become jealous and sabotage your business. Do you believe in the same God? Do you worship him in similar ways? These are often overlooked characteristics, but they can have a major impact on whether or not your business prospers.

Some differences are good. Some weaknesses you can tolerate by having strengths in other areas. Some you should never overlook.

Starting out slow not only gives you time to learn your business, it gives you time to learn about yourself and your partner. It also gives you time to see how God is building into you what you need to move forward. My husband and I were considering joining forces with another couple on a business venture, until my husband saw the other husband, smoking crack! That was a shock and a deal breaker. It was time to pray and seek God's guidance. Certainly, God is able to break the bondage of a crack addiction, and for the addict, that must take priority over starting a business.

Sometimes people draw near to you, because they are running from something or somebody. It is important to know what their baggage is and how much of it you can carry. Everybody has some baggage including you. In my life, I have discovered that I can see the vision clearly and how to get there, but I do not always see the opposition from people who should be on my side. It is important to me to collaborate with people who are gifted at discerning danger behind smiles. **It is a wonderful thing to have a partner that adds to you**. It is burdensome to have one that does not. It is important to nourish the gifts that God has placed in each of you so they will spring up and blossom.

Therefore, here is my suggestion:

- make an honest list of your strengths and weaknesses
- make a list of strengths and weaknesses you want in a partner
- Do your partner's strengths compliment your weaknesses?
- Do your strengths compliment his or her weaknesses?
- Pray about this and ask God to help you identify the right person.
- Then leave it alone
- Trust God to bring the right person at the right time.
- As you continue building your business, people will appear.
- As you get to know them, refer back to your list
- Honestly evaluate whether they meet the criteria

- You do not have the right to remake someone into what you need them to be
- In your alone time with God, ask Him if this is the right person to partner with
- Wait for an answer
- Have the courage to follow God

LEGAL STRUCTURE

The legal structure of your business will become important when your business becomes profitable and starts gaining assets. It is important to consult a lawyer and a tax advisor for guidance on which structure will work best for you. There are six main forms of business structures. The details of these entities are beyond the scope of this book, but a few key points are listed below:

1. A **sole proprietorship** is the way most very small businesses start. It is easy, quick, and cheap. It usually requires less than twenty dollars to register the business' name. For tax purposes, you report the business' profits and losses on your personal tax return. You are personally responsible for all the liabilities of the business, which a creditor could collect from your personal assets if you have any. For that reason, it is generally not advisable to stay a sole proprietorship once your business is up and running.
2. A **General Partnership** is where two or more people own the business jointly. Each partner is responsible for all of the liabilities of the business and if a debt is due, a creditor could collect the full amount from the partner that is the easiest to collect from regardless of who made the debt. The partners report profits and losses on their tax returns according to their percent of ownership.
3. A **limited partnership** must have at least one general partner and one limited partner. The general partner has personal liability for all liabilities of the partnership. The limited partner is a "silent

partner", does not have personal liability for the business, and cannot take part in the management. The partners report profits and losses on their tax returns according to their percent of ownership.

4. A **Limited Liability Partnership** (LLP) is similar to a general partnership, except the partners are only liable for their own negligence.
5. A **corporation** is a separate entity. The shareholders own it. They are also called stockholders. A corporation can have only one shareholder or an unlimited amount. It can be taxed, sued, and enter into contracts. In most cases, creditors cannot collect from the owners' personal assets to cover the company's liabilities. The corporation files it own tax return. In most very small businesses, the owner(s) work for the company and are paid a salary.
    a. The owners may choose to elect "S Corporation" status. In that case, the corporation is taxed like a partnership and the owners report the profits and losses of the S Corporation on their personal tax returns. They are still protected from the liabilities of the company.
6. A **Limited Liability Company** (LLC) is a hybrid of a corporation and a partnership. When you form the company, you choose whether the company will be taxed like a partnership or taxed like a corporation. The owners and any officers and directors are protected from the liabilities of the company.

ADVISORS

As your business grows, you will need to start building relationships with key professionals to advise you. They include people in your particular trade, an accountant, lawyer, insurance agent, and banker. Their job will be to advise you, not teach you how to run your business. That is your job and one that you will always be learning how to do better.

Expect to pay your advisors well. **Pray about who you are to let advise you**, weight the information you receive, move cautiously. Overtime, you will know whom you can trust. Proverbs 11:14 NAS says, *Where there is no guidance the people fall, But in the abundance of counselors there is victory.*

Some of your best advisors may be people you never meet, personally. They can mentor you through books, sermons, seminars, or even movies. Many knowledgeable people will not have time to sit with you one on one. You will have to glean information. There is plenty of information available. There is no excuse to be ignorant. Information is important to your success. There is a battle for your mind and you must fight the temptation to give up or indulge in counterproductive behaviors. Nevertheless, if you do stumble and fall, you can get up and keep on learning.

HIRING EMPLOYEES

Many Christian business owners have compassion for people. We are moved by the struggles of people and their requests for jobs. If we are not careful, we could easily end up hiring people that cannot help us. Then we end up carrying them and paying for it with more than money. This does neither of us any good. One of the worst things to do is to hire unqualified people for a job and expect them to step up to the plate. Even worse is to hire friends and family that are too familiar with you and do not or will not recognize your authority as the boss even of your own company. Learning how to hire and work people effectively is an art that is learned.

First, you have to decide what you want them to do. **If you do not define the job for your employees, they will define it for you. If you are not happy with their definition, you will probably end up firing them or they will quit at a critical moment.** It is not enough to say you just want someone to answer the phone. Answer the phone and say what? If you hire someone and all they do is answer the phones while you do everything else you will get angry with them while they sit idle and wait for the phones to ring. If you hire someone to simply answer the phones and take down the name and number of the person who called and no messages, you will get even angrier when you stop what you are doing to call someone back and all they wanted to know was something simple like your address. The point is you, as the owner, must have a plan for your staff just as you have for your business.

In the case of the vendor business, you may need someone to help you find and book marketplaces, help find appropriate products according to your guidelines, place orders and track them, track inventory and help with financial records, travel to events to help set up, sell and take down. You may need someone to help you with all of this or some portions of it. You must make it clear what you need and then hire someone that is able to do all that you need.

You will have to research similar job descriptions and determine a fair wage. If you offer too low of salary, qualified people will look somewhere else. **Most employees feel that they are not paid enough and most employers feel that they are paying too much.** You have to account for all your expenses when determining a salary. If you take too much money out of your business to pay salaries, no one is helped when the business goes bankrupt. There must be money left in the business for unexpected expenses. If the computer quits working, the employees will expect you to buy another one. If the air conditioning needs repairing, they will look to you to have it fixed and still expect their full salary.

Most new employers do not account for the additional taxes that must be paid on their employee's wages. Before you hire someone, think through all these issues. Consider if you can invest in technology to make your job easier instead of hiring someone. Evaluate the profitability of your tasks. Sometimes, employees push you faster and harder than you want to go because you are trying to make enough money to pay them. You do not need to make every sale and satisfy every customer. Some customers are not yours. They do not fit with your spirit or goals. You have to have the courage to walk away or tell them no. Some employees even family and friends cannot go where you are going. God has not called them to the same place and in the same season that He has called you. You have to have courage to let them go to their destiny and you must go to yours. One of the greatest benefits to being an entrepreneur is the freedom to choose with whom you will do business and with whom you will pay to be in your workspace as an employee. You are the boss. You must make the decision and accept responsibility.

LEASING RETAIL SPACE

Leasing retail space is a pivotal step for most small businesses. You have grown beyond the capacity of your home and have gone from part-time to full-time. If this is not the case, you are not yet ready to lease. **A common mistake that small business owners make is to make this move too soon without counting the cost**. Expect to pay two months' rent, a deposit, plus your share of the property taxes, insurance and common maintenance area called the triple nets. Expect to pay a great deal more than the monthly rent just to walk through the doors with lights and phones. For example if the rent is $1000 per month, expect to pay at least $5000 as follows:

Two months' rent	$2000
Rent deposit	$1000
Triple Nets	$400
Electricity deposit	$200
Water deposit	$100
Telephone deposit	$200
Building occupancy fee	$50
Sign permits, etc	$50
Phone system	$500
Signs	$1000
	$5500

You will still need to buy inventory, furniture and fixtures, computers, cash register, industry specific licenses, advertising, credit card machines, and the list goes on. Expect to do a lot of the work yourself. You can negotiate the lease with the property manager if you have a lot of remodeling to do, but **Do not try to negotiate the initial payments. It looks bad in the business world**. It says to people, "I don't have enough money now, but I'm hoping that by the time the next payment comes due, I'll somehow have the money." It makes you appear to be an extremely unstable risk. It is better to wait until you have the money to pay the initial costs and negotiate future payments. The property manager will probably negotiate the next two months free. You move in on January 1, and the next rent will be due by April 1. The lease should contain any special agreements from you or the property manager.

Location, Location, Location

Where you lease must be consistent with the type of business you have. Study how neighborhood oriented businesses group themselves together. They are strategically located on main streets between homes and highways that people travel on going to and from work. Malls are usually located off freeways for easy access. Office buildings tend to clump together in business centers. Medical offices tend to cluster around hospitals.

How will your customers find you? If your business depends on walk in or drive up traffic, you must position it so people can see it easily as they drive by. **Most people travel the same routes repeatedly. They make mental notes of the signs and stores they see along the way.** If you choose an out of the way place because the rent is cheap, you will spend much more money on advertising than you would have spent renting a place on a main street. In addition, you want an address connected to a main street that people can find easily.

You should drive to different areas in different parts of town to get a feel for how your business would fit there. How many other businesses are there that are already doing what you do? Some markets are already overly saturated and competition is fierce. If you have a high-end product, do not rent in a discount center that attracts bargain hunters. Is the area growing or declining? You can study the demographics of an area by simply typing in a zip code on the Internet.

How far do you want to travel from home each day? You are likely to be at the location you choose for a long time. Do you like the neighborhood? Do you feel a sense of connection with the community? **In the beginning you may be working long hours, is it safe?** What are the opening and closing times of the surrounding businesses? This is an often-overlooked point, but their hours will affect yours.

Parking is another overlooked area. How much parking do you need for customers? Will they need to park for a long time or will they be in and out? How much parking are the neighboring businesses using? If you attract customers that are in and out in ten minutes, but the next-door beauty shop's customers take all the parking spaces for several hours, your potential customers are likely to keep driving and find a competitor with available parking. This could have a devastating impact on your business that you did not anticipate.

How will you pay your rent until your business is able to make enough money to pay it? How will you cover your other expenses? You need to put a plan together long before you sign the lease. By this time, you should have a working budget. Can you bring the customers you already have into your new location? Ask them, but do not depend on them. You will have to attract new customers.

PROFESSIONALISM

As God brings you into the light, remember to glorify Him in all you do. Operate a professional business from the start. Have business cards, advertisements, and signs made by a professional printer. Keep your environment clean and neat at all times. Furniture and fixtures should match the surroundings and each other. There should not be clutter. Place storage behind walls or partitions out of the view of the customer. Speak in a professional and friendly tone. Dress professionally and appropriately for your business.

Love should abound in all that you do. It should be your atmosphere. Play gentle music, preferably Christian. Maintain a temperature that is comfortable for your customers. If your business is family oriented, your environment should be safe and durable enough for children. Phone etiquette is essential. Answer the phone on the second or third ring. Invest in a nice phone system that will play music while you have customers on hold. People will disrespect your business if it looks and sounds unprofessional. Professionalism is not about buying expensive things that you cannot afford. It is self-awareness. It tells others how to receive you, and how you will receive them. It comes from the inside not the outside.

Key Points to Remember

- God will call you out of obscurity
- He will dress you in the appropriate wedding clothes
- Choosing a partner requires knowledge, wisdom, and prayer
- Seek professional guidance on the legal structure of your business
- Define the job description and determine the salary before you hire
- Consider all your options before leasing a retail space, you are likely to be there for a long time
- Honor God in your business

Conclusion

But seek ye first the kingdom of God,
and his righteousness;

and all these things shall be added unto you.

Matthew 6:33

Conclusion

There is no greater love in the entire world than the love of God manifested in Christ Jesus. It is a love that transcends time and space. It speaks to our inner most parts and makes believe in the inconceivable. It is a simple concept and yet volumes upon volumes of books have been written to try to explain it. In the end, it cannot be received though our intellect it must be received through faith. Jesus said faith could move mountains. You have to ask yourself, do I really have the faith to believe? Can I really be all that God has called me to be? Does He really know me? Will He really help me? Can I really rise up out of my situation? Will it really work for me? No one can answer these questions for you but God.

In Matthew 7: 7-12 NIV, Jesus said

"Ask and it will be given to you; seek and you will find; knock and the door will be opened to you.

For everyone who asks receives; he who seeks finds; and to him who knocks, the door will be opened.

"Which of you, if his son asks for bread, will give him a stone?

Or if he asks for a fish, will give him a snake?

If you, then, though you are evil, know how to give good gifts to your children, how much more will your Father in heaven give good gifts to those who ask him!

So in everything, do to others what you would have them do to you, for this sums up the Law and the Prophets.

In John 6:27-40 NIV, Jesus said,

Do not work for food that spoils, but for food that endures to eternal life, which the Son of Man will give you. On him God the Father has placed his seal of approval."

Then they asked him, "What must we do to do the works God requires?" Jesus answered, "The work of God is this: to believe in the one he has sent."

So they asked him, "What miraculous sign then will you give that we may see it and believe you? What will you do?

Our forefathers ate the manna in the desert; as it is written: 'He gave them bread from heaven to eat.'"

Jesus said to them, "I tell you the truth, it is not Moses who has given you the bread from heaven, but it is my Father who gives you the true bread from heaven.

For the bread of God is he who comes down from heaven and gives life to the world."

"Sir," they said, "from now on give us this bread."

Then Jesus declared, "I am the bread of life. He who comes to me will never go hungry, and he who believes in me will never be thirsty.

But as I told you, you have seen me and still you do not believe.

All that the Father gives me will come to me, and whoever comes to me I will never drive away.

For I have come down from heaven not to do my will but to do the will of him who sent me.

And this is the will of him who sent me, that I shall lose none of all that he has given me, but raise them up at the last day.

For my Father's will is that everyone who looks to the Son and believes in him shall have eternal life, and I will raise him up at the last day."

If you seek after God with your whole heart, you will find Him. He will answer your deepest questions and give you good gifts. Jesus said *all* that the Father gives to Him will never go hungry or thirsty and He will never drive them away. In addition, He will raise us up at the last day and we will have eternal life.

Remember, you need supernatural and natural knowledge in order to grow. You have to continue to learn about the kingdom of God as well as business. Continue to set measurable and achievable goals. Pat yourself on the back frequently, and learn from your mistakes, keep updating your products or services, stay ahead of the crowd, and keep looking for ways to improve. Sometimes subtle improvements make a big difference. You cannot afford to get so comfortable with a product or place that you fail to realize the seasons are changing. *There is a time for everything, and a season for every activity under heaven, Ecclesiastes 3:1.*

On the other hand, you cannot be frantic. You must settle down, let the peace of God live in you, and guide you. Pause frequently and communicate with God. You have received exactly what God intended for you to receive for this season of your life. He has been stirring up the gifts within you leading you to the next level of your life. This is just the beginning. God is standing ready to release ten thousand angels to help you with whatever you need. You can go as far as you can believe.

Ultimately, there is no lasting success without God. **Even if your business survives your lifetime, your soul will perish without God**. We build businesses, but our main objective is to build the kingdom of God. Our money will multiply if we put it to work. Jesus said it would. Precious souls will be saved, if we let our light shine and glorify our father, which is in Heaven. God has given us His holy spirit to live in us and guide us into all truths. We have to remain prayerful and grateful for all that He has entrusted to us.

If you hang on in there, **one day you will reach a place where you are no longer struggling**. Your profits will begin to soar far beyond your expenses. You will have gained valuable experience and learned more than you ever thought you could. You will look back at the hard times and know that it had to be God that brought you through.

People will begin to recognize you as a community leader and a mighty man or woman of God. They will ask you how you did it and listen to your answer. You will notice that you have moved ahead of all the people that seemed to have had so much when you were struggling. You will understand the story of Joseph on much deeper level. You will be grateful to God, not arrogant. You will be dressed in the appropriate wedding clothes. You will be a builder in the kingdom of God.

It is time to complete your business plan. Find a format that works for you and put it in writing. Whenever possible, help the less fortunate. Have fun and enjoy your life!

Appendix

QUICK SCRIPTURE REFERENCE

Chapter One

But seek ye first the kingdom of God, and his righteousness; and all these things shall be added unto you.
Matthew 6:33

Therefore whosoever heareth these sayings of mine, and doeth them, I will liken him unto a wise man, which built his house upon a rock:
And the rain descended, and the floods came, and the winds blew, and beat upon that house; and it fell not: for it was founded upon a rock.
And every one that heareth these sayings of mine, and doeth them not, shall be likened unto a foolish man, which built his house upon the sand:
And the rain descended, and the floods came, and the winds blew, and beat upon that house; and it fell: and great was the fall of it.
And it came to pass, when Jesus had ended these sayings, the people were astonished at his doctrine:
For he taught them as one having authority, and not as the scribes.
Matthew 7:24-29

But the people that do know their God shall be strong and do exploits.
Daniel 11:32

In the beginning was the Word, and the Word was with God, and the Word was God.
The same was in the beginning with God.
All things were made by Him; and without him was not anything made that was made.
In Him was life; and the life was the light of men.
And the light shineth in the darkness; and the darkness comprehended it not.
There was a man sent from God, whose name John.
The same came for a witness, to bear witness of the Light, that all men through him might believe.
He was not that Light, but was sent to bear witness of that light

That was the true light, which lighteth every man that cometh into the world.
He was in the world, and the world was made by Him, and the world Knew Him not.
He came unto His own, and His own received him not.
But as many as received Him, to them gave He <u>power to become</u> the sons of God, even to them that believed on his name:
Which were born, not of blood, nor of the will of the flesh, nor the will of man, but of God.
And the Word was made flesh, and dwelt among us, (and we beheld his glory, the glory as of the only begotten of the Father,) full of grace and truth.
John 1:1-14

all power is given unto me in heaven and in earth.
Matthew 28:18

behold, the Lord thy God hath set the land before thee: go up and possess it, as the Lord God of thy fathers hath said unto thee; fear not, neither be discouraged.
Deuteronomy 1:21

people are destroyed for a lack of knowledge.
Hosea 4:6

Then they brought little children to Him, that He might touch them; but the disciples rebuked those who brought them.
But when Jesus saw it, He was greatly displeased and said to them, Let the little children come to Me, and do not forbid them; for of such is the kingdom of God.
Assuredly, I say to you, whoever does not receive the kingdom of God as a little child will by no means enter it.
And He took them up in His arms, laid His hands on them, and blessed them.
Mark 10:13-16

But as many as received Him, to them He gave the right to become children of God, even to those who believe in His name
John 1:12.

do you see a man diligent in his business? He shall stand before kings; he shall not stand before obscure men.
Proverbs 22:29

The story of Joseph
Genesis 37-48

Chapter Two

... the kingdom of heaven suffereth violence and the violent take it by force
Matthew 11:12

who hath ears to hear, let him hear
Matthew 13:9

Whereunto shall we liken the kingdom of God? Or with what comparison shall we compare it?
It is like a grain of mustard seed, which, when it is sown in the earth, is less than all the seeds that be in the earth:
But when it is sown, it groweth up, and becomes greater that all herbs, and shooteth out great branches; so that the fowls of the air may lodge under the shadow of it.
Mark 4:30-32

one can chase a thousand and two can put ten thousand to flight
Deuteronomy 32:30

Chapter Three

"*Go! I am sending you out like lambs among wolves,*" Luke 10:3 NIV
"I saw Satan fall like lightning from heaven," Luke10:18 NIV.
Verse 17 said the *seventy-two returned with joy.*

Chapter Four

By wisdom a house is built, and through understanding it is established, through knowledge it rooms are filled.
Proverbs 24:3

Chapter Five

A certain nobleman went into a far country to receive for himself a kingdom, and to return.
And he called his ten servants, and delivered them a pound, and said unto them, Occupy till I come.
But his citizens hated him, and sent a message after him, saying, We will not have this man to reign over us.
And it came to pass, that when he returned, having received his kingdom, then he commanded these servants to be called unto him, to whom he had given the money, that he might know how much every man had gained by trading.
Then came the first, saying, Lord thy pound has gained ten pounds.
And he said unto him Well, thou good servant: Because thou has been faithful in a very little have thou authority over ten cities.
And the second came, saying, Lord, thy pound hath gained five pounds.
And he said likewise to him, Be thou also over five cities.
And another came, saying, Lord, Behold, here is thy pound, which I have kept laid up in a napkin:
For I feared thee, because thou art an austere man: thou takest up that thou layedst not down, and reapest that thou didst not sow.
And he said unto him, Out of thine own mouth will I judge thee, thou wicked servant. Thou knewest that I was an austere man, taking up that I laid not down, and reaping that I did not sow:
Wherefore then gavest not thou my money into the bank, that at my coming I might have required mine own with usury?
And he said unto them that stood by, Take from him the pound, and give it to him that hath ten pounds.
And they said unto him, Lord, he hath ten pounds.
For I say unto you, That unto every one which hath shall be given, and from him that hath not, even that he hath shall be taken away from him.

But those mine enemies, which would not that I should reign over them, bring hither, and slay them before me."
Luke 19: 12-27

No man also seweth a piece of new cloth on an old garment: else the new piece that filled it up taketh away from the old, and the rent is made worse.
And no man putteth new wine into old bottles: else the new wine doth burst the bottles, and the wine is spilled, and the bottles will be marred: but new wine must be put into new bottles.
Mark 2:21-22

I will stand upon my watch, and set me upon the tower, and will watch to see what He will say unto me, and what I shall answer when I am reproved.
And the Lord answered me, and said, write the vision, and make it plain upon tablets, that he may run that readeth it.
For the vision is yet for an appointed time, but at the end it shall speak, and not lie: though it tarry, wait for it; because it will surely come, it will not tarry.
Habakkuk 2:1-3

for I know the thoughts I think toward you, saith the Lord, thoughts of peace, and not of evil, to give you an expected end.
Then shall ye call upon me, and ye shall go and pray unto me, and I will harken unto you.
Jeremiah 29:11

When the unclean spirit is gone out of man, he walketh through dry places, seeking rest; and finding none, he saith, I will return unto my house from whence I came out.
And when he cometh, he findeth it swept and garnished.
Then goeth he, and taketh to him seven other spirits more wicked that himself: and they enter in, and dwell there: and the last state of the man is worse than the first.
Luke 11:24-26

Half of the men worked, while the other half were equipped with spears, bows, and armor.
The officers posted themselves behind all the people of Judah who were building the wall.
Those who carried materials did their work with one hand and held a weapon in the other, and each of the builders wore his sword at his side as he worked.
Nehemiah 4:16-18

If you confess with your mouth Jesus as Lord, and believe in your heart that God raised Him from the dead, you will be saved. For with the heart a person believes and with the mouth confesses, resulting in salvation.
Romans 10:9-10

Everyone who calls on the name of the Lord will be saved.
Joel 2:32

Chapter Six

Ye are the light of the world. A city that is set on an hill cannot be hid.
Neither do men light a candle, and put it under a bushel, but on a candlestick; and it giveth light unto all that are in the house.
Let your light so shine before men, that they may see your good works, and glorify your Father, which is in heaven.
Matthew 6:14-16 ASV

The kingdom of heaven is like a certain king who arranged a marriage for his son,
and sent out his servants to call those who were invited to the wedding; and they were not willing to come.
Again, he sent out other servants, saying, Tell those who are invited, See, I have prepared my dinner; my oxen and fatted cattle are killed, and all things are ready. Come to the wedding.
But they made light of it and went their ways, one to his own farm, another to his business.
And the rest seized his servants, treated them spitefully, and killed them.

But when the king heard about it, he was furious. And he sent out his armies, destroyed those murderers, and burned up their city.
Then he said to his servants, 'The wedding is ready, but those who were invited were not worthy.
Therefore go into the highways, and as many as you find, invite to the wedding.
So those servants went out into the highways and gathered together all whom they found, both bad and good. And the wedding hall was filled with guests.
But when the king came in to see the guests, he saw a man there who did not have on a wedding garment.
So he said to him, Friend, how did you come in here without a wedding garment? And he was speechless.
Then the king said to the servants, Bind him hand and foot, take him away, and cast him into outer darkness; there will be weeping and gnashing of teeth.
For many are called, but few are chosen.
Matthew 22:1-14

Where there is no guidance the people fall, But in the abundance of counselors there is victory.
Proverbs 11:14 NAS

Conclusion

"Ask and it will be given to you; seek and you will find; knock and the door will be opened to you.
For everyone who asks receives; he who seeks finds; and to him who knocks, the door will be opened.
"Which of you, if his son asks for bread, will give him a stone?
Or if he asks for a fish, will give him a snake?
If you, then, though you are evil, know how to give good gifts to your children, how much more will your Father in heaven give good gifts to those who ask him!
So in everything, do to others what you would have them do to you, for this sums up the Law and the Prophets.
Matthew 7: 7-12 NIV

Do not work for food that spoils, but for food that endures to eternal life, which the Son of Man will give you. On him God the Father has placed his seal of approval."
Then they asked him, "What must we do to do the works God requires?"
Jesus answered, "The work of God is this: to believe in the one he has sent."
So they asked him, "What miraculous sign then will you give that we may see it and believe you? What will you do?
Our forefathers ate the manna in the desert; as it is written: 'He gave them bread from heaven to eat.'"
Jesus said to them, "I tell you the truth, it is not Moses who has given you the bread from heaven, but it is my Father who gives you the true bread from heaven.
For the bread of God is he who comes down from heaven and gives life to the world."
"Sir," they said, "from now on give us this bread."
Then Jesus declared, "I am the bread of life. He who comes to me will never go hungry, and he who believes in me will never be thirsty.
But as I told you, you have seen me and still you do not believe.
All that the Father gives me will come to me, and whoever comes to me I will never drive away.
For I have come down from heaven not to do my will but to do the will of him who sent me.
And this is the will of him who sent me, that I shall lose none of all that he has given me, but raise them up at the last day.
For my Father's will is that everyone who looks to the Son and believes in him shall have eternal life, and I will raise him up at the last day."
John 6:27-40 NIV

There is a time for everything, and a season for every activity under heaven
Ecclesiastes 3:1

To contact the author write to:

Freda Wallace

430 N Main St

Duncanville, TX 75116

978-0-595-44452-6
0-595-44452-0

LaVergne, TN USA
29 October 2009
162404LV00002B/1/A